The Fur Beneath My Wings

Our Relationship with Animals and the Valuable Lessons They Teach Us

HARTFORD J. HOUGH

ISBN 13:978-1976046254

ISBN 10: 1976046254

Dedication

For Guffington and Mr. Belvedere

Acknowledgements

First and foremost, I want to give honor and praise to my Lord and Savior Jesus Christ. Writing this book has been a labor of love, and every day, He has shown me His love and mercy by allowing me to complete this task. I thank Him for placing it in my heart to do and for seeing me through until its completion. Though the book is completed, this is just the beginning of the work. God has been so good to me, and for all things, I say "to God be all the glory for the great things He has done!"

I want to thank my family. This would include the spirits of my mother and father, my grandparents, aunts, uncles, cousins, nieces, nephews, and great-nephews. Your unconditional love and support mean everything to me. In particular, my two nieces, Deidre and Carolyn. You always believed in me and have availed yourselves to me through time and distance. I will always love you for that and for being who you both are. Carolyn and Sammy would be proud.

The list of my friends could read like an encyclopedia. Where do I begin, and where do I end? For me, this would almost seem insurmountable, but I will do my best here:

I want to thank my dear friend, Edwinia Finley, for your constant support, inspiration, and "extra push" in seeing the work is finished. You are my big sister, and I am so grateful God allowed our paths to cross and birth such a wonderful friendship. You, too, are my family. And your family has become mine as well. It was an arduous task, but we did it, my friend. We are both elevated to say we are "people who know people."

To Connie Stewart, a dear friend and woman of undying faith. Our friendship blossomed over the years when we both discovered the artists in each other. It was here you gave me support, encouragement, love, and friendship. Our phone calls and letters through the years have been a true testament of our friendship. You believed in me when, at times, I didn't believe in myself. Thank you for just being you.

To Simone, a unique bond and special friendship. "Girl, you know what we've been through, and we can look around and say, 'but God.'" We stood together, faith to faith, and when the odds were stacked against us, we still came out victorious. The attacks on our friendship have been many, but God delivered us out of them all. Thank you for hanging in there with me.

To Juanita "Nene" Edwards, you have become my sister from another mother. What began at 294 Greene Avenue with a simple introduction became a bond of love, support, and encouragement through the years. Always having my back and making sure I didn't "go rogue on the people," and helping me keep it one hundred. You respected my faith and position in life and never gave me reason to doubt. You know I love you, Arturo, Renaldo, and Kathy, and my extended family to life.

To my god-sister, Lakiesta "Kiki" Evans, and my family in Little Rock, Arkansas. Mother Wonda Faye, Dominique, Tia, Shimika, Keeona, Yashika, "the prayers of the righteous availeth much," and I know some praying came out of Arkansas for your brother. You all hold a special place in my heart, and I will always treasure that one Thanksgiving that gave me a "new" family. Love you much!

To MJ McGlen, my friend and writing coach. Thank you for being the catalyst to getting this project done and for believing in me. You and Keith are the best!

To my places of employment and the people that helped shape my career and gave me a platform to "make room for my gifts." Morgan Stanley, Sotheby's International Realty, Universal

Studios, Ajilon Professionals, and all the wonderful people I have known. Your support, love, kindness, and encouragement have been a "jewel in my heart." Thank you.

To my "Sunday Brunch Crew," Val, Deborah, Latrease, Robert, Beatrice, and Adrienne. We have formed this unique group of friends that love to share, laugh, and have a good meal. You have all been such a blessing to me, and I love you all. Even if I mess up the reservation or get the directions wrong, you will never put me out of "The Temptations" (inside humor).

To the graduating class of Bishop Loughlin MHS 1983. Why would anyone want to thank their high school graduating class, you may ask? I graduated with a very special group of people. Over the years, we have grown and matured in many areas of our lives. We are married, have children, grandchildren, relationships, careers, and trials and tribulations, but we always manage to reconnect and come back to that place that brought us together in 1979. We are all successful in our own right, and we are better for having known (and still know) each other. Go, Loughlin!

To my Howard University family. Many friendships were formed on "The Yard" and have remained strong and resilient through the years. We became what we all dreamed we could be, and our experience at this HBCU made us better. No matter how far we go in life, Howard will always be a part of us. Keep on keeping on, my brothers and sisters.

To all the places of faith and the people that had a part in my spiritual growth and development, as a man and as a man of God. Ebenezer Baptist Church, Antioch Baptist Church, Brooklyn Tabernacle Deliverance Center, Bridge Street AME Church, Evangel Church (formerly Evangel Temple), Greater Mount Calvary Holy Church, and Hollywood United Methodist

Church and Faith Fellowship. My journey of faith has had many participants who have taught, encouraged, supported, and inspired me throughout the years. We have prayed, fasted, studied scripture, sang, gone on retreats, grown in ministry, excelled in leadership, and beat the enemy upside the head every step of the way. We are blessed, victorious, and, yes, highly favored.

Foreword

Every so often, a book comes along that captures the heart of the reader. In *The Fur Beneath My Wings: Our Relationship with Animals and the Valuable Lessons They Teach Us*, Hartford has a unique way of tugging at your heartstrings by including our "furry friends" in his inspirational-style writing about some of life's most penetrating circumstances. Hartford's love for animals exudes continuously throughout each chapter. Whether addressing an emotional topic, teaching a lesson on love or offering a message of hope and inspiration, you will relish in every subject as each pooch or feline friend is introduced and becomes a part of the pivotal point of the message.

Since our high school days at Bishop Loughlin Memorial High School in Brooklyn, New York, Hartford always had a heart and a love for all living things. His sensitivity, quick wit, and zest for life were infectious! Because he always brought joy to the hearts of others, it was no surprise to me that he would be the author of such an inspirational and thought-provoking book that would uniquely include the animals that are so near and dear to his heart.

While reading, I recollected my experience with both the love and the loss of a dog. It was at the age of twelve that I lost my beloved dog, Coffee, to a car accident. This was my very first experience with a loss in my life. The penetrating pain that I experienced was one that would never be forgotten. However, this experience also brought to light the intensity of love and how powerful love can truly be. Throughout his literary artwork, Hartford sheds new insight on the emotional attributes that animals contribute to human lives.

When one takes on the responsibility of owning and rearing a pet, it becomes more than just an animal in your home — he or she becomes a treasured family member. Let's face it, pets are far more than cute, little creatures. They serve as true companions who have the ability to replace the loneliness in our lives with joy and happiness. Their unconditional love and lack of judgement can reduce the stress of any given circumstance. Just think about it, what better greeting than to open your front door after a rough day in the office and be elatedly hailed by a wagging-tailed buddy who erases the memory of that unreasonable boss or the person who scuffed your new designer shoes on an overcrowded subway train!

The Fur Beneath My Wings: Our Relationship with Animals and the Valuable Lessons They Teach Us is an inspirational book that will touch your heart, help you heal emotionally, and cause you to rethink some of your fondest memories.

As a certified family life educator, fellow author, and most importantly a former pet owner, I connected with Hartford's magnificent work on many levels. No matter the circumstances, life's challenges are seemingly easier to manage and fond memories are ever present when you have experienced the unconditional love of a pet, at least, once in your lifetime.

Wen Robins, MA, CFLE
Certified Family Life Educator, Life Coach, Author

Table of Contents

Introduction

(Everything has a Purpose)

Life has an interesting way of teaching you a lesson. God, being the author and giver of life, will use its challenges and experiences to show you the reason there is existence in your life. I believe we all want to know what our purpose is for being here, and finding that out makes going through life a little easier. It gives us a greater sense of direction. It gives us clarity by letting us know why we are here and what we are supposed to be doing.

I have always been a man with animals. I have loved them since my childhood, and even now, they hold a striking presence in my life. I have come to look at animals as not just animals. They are living, breathing creatures that are here for a significant purpose, just as humans are. God created them for a reason, and once you come to understand that reason, you will appreciate our friends from the animal kingdom that much more. You will not just see Fluffy as a cat meandering around the house, looking to get into some trouble. Duke will not just be the little canine wagging his tail and barking endlessly. You will see that their little lives, precious as they are, have valuable meaning.

Many who know me have equated me with one of my many blessed gifts. I am an accomplished baker and have been doing so for over thirty years. So the thought of a baker writing a book about animals and life lessons might seem a bit far-fetched, but it is not really, when you consider the plan of God for my life. He has designed and created me for the many wonderful things I shall accomplish in this life before my time is over. Discovering a newfound purpose and walking in it is just a part of the plan.

I have come to love animals with a passion that dictates my actions toward them. I want to bring this level of awareness to others.

Animals are here for the purpose of teaching us. As humans, we are subject to human error and make a lot of mistakes in this human experience. Animals serve a single purpose, and their focus is to be who they are and embody the lessons we as humans should know and be practicing. You can take, for example, unconditional love. How many of us can say we love another person unconditionally? This means you love them in spite of themselves, faults and all. Their temperament, attitude, and feelings in a situation do not make your love for them waver. Why? Because it is unconditional. Animals know this and seem to practice it effortlessly, and the beauty of their presence is that all they want to do is love you. How wonderful is that?

As man examines his purpose, he does not often consider the things in and around him. Sometimes, he is oblivious to the fact that everything in this world serves a purpose. Whether it is to be used as a resource and sustainable form of life or the basic presence of a tree in the middle of a park. In life, sadly, we take so much for granted. We do it so often that we soon forget that we are taking precious things around us for granted. Many of us see people with their pets and we smile. We wistfully pass them by, thinking how nice it is the person has a pet to care for in their life. We don't ponder it so deeply that the little creature they possess is in their life for a specific reason. The reason is unbeknownst to you, but is fulfilling in and of itself for the person and their animal. In the handiwork of God's creation, these two lives have been placed together, and the fulfillment of their relationship lies in the purpose for which they were both created.

I am reminded of the story in the Bible about the woman with the issue of blood. Many of us are familiar with it and have heard it preached and taught countless times. We know this woman had an ailment for twelve long years. She was unceremoniously unclean and was probably isolated due to her condition. We know she also possessed great faith. Her faith was so strong that all she wanted to do was touch the hem of Jesus's garment. Have you ever thought about this fact: What was her name? She did have a name. Because we don't think about it, we just don't regard it as being that important. Yet it is. It is the same with animals. We don't regard them as being anything more than animals, but they are just as important as anything God has created, from man to angels, to the skies and seas. And because it is God's pleasure to both will and to do, we know their presence is not by happenstance.

I was fascinated to learn an interesting fact about turtles. The average turtle can live up to eighty years old! There have been turtles who have outlived my own family and friends. It is good to know that God has given them such longevity. Their lives serve a significant purpose and message for us all. We often think about turtles as just being slow and useless. However, a key lesson I have learned from them is that life is not a sprint, but a marathon. It is a long, arduous journey, but if you hang in there long enough, you will eventually reach your goal and destination. Isn't that something to garner such a lesson from a simple reptile that you probably gave no more thought to than yesterday's newspaper. Yet, turtles are here. They are a part of God's plan and His purpose.

It is with this frame of mind that I enter into writing *The Fur Beneath My Wings*, which is a compilation of stories from my own personal experiences, as well as other shared stories, about the relationship that mankind has with animals. While we occupy space here together, we must co-exist in a way that brings productive harmony. We must learn to appreciate and value animals' lives as well as those of our fellow human beings. We must treat them with kindness and respect just as we would our neighbors and friends. Their place here is no less important than the man you don't know laying in the street. A living creature, be it animal or human, has great value and worth. When we have mastered this lesson, then, and only then, can we live in a world that exudes peace, love, and harmony.

Chapter 1: Why Worry?

A Lesson in Learning not to Worry

"Look at the birds of the air, for they neither sow nor reap nor gather into barns; yet your heavenly Father feeds them. Are not you of more value than they? Which of you by worrying can add one cubit to his stature? So why do you worry about clothing? Consider the lilies of the field, how they grow: they neither toil nor spin, and yet I say to you that even Solomon in all his glory was not arrayed like one of these. Now if God so clothes the grass of the field, which today is, and tomorrow is thrown into the oven, will He not much more clothe you, O you of little faith?"
Matthew 6:26-30

How much time do we spend worrying about things we have no control over? The answer to this question is obvious — too much! Life gives us so many challenges, and how we go about handling those challenges is totally up to us. We can allow these "tests" to overwhelm us to the point that we fall under its magnitude, or we can manage the test, and come out on the other side, stronger and wiser. How wonderful it would be if we could live the carefree life and not have to worry about anything that befalls us. As human beings, we do not have that luxury. We have the intelligence and wherewithal to deal with challenges. Yet, we still worry ourselves into states of frenzy and hectic despair.

Consider the birds. As I stood on the ledge of the subway platform one warm spring day, where the clouds were overcast, and a light coolness was in the air, I watched them. There was a team of seagulls flying overhead. They looked so free as they took flight and painted the sky with the tapestry of their wings. They were quiet in their ascent, yet there was a volume to their presence. From the moment I saw them, the sky was theirs. They owned it in a way that we, as humans, often miss when it comes to ownership. They did not lapse in their flight, and they were deliberate in their actions. They were in the sky, and it was magnificent.

I watched them as they flew back and forth, and I was struck by this one aspect of their flight. They did not seem to have a care in the world. As they flew, a light mist started to fall, and they seemed to bathe in its cool, refreshing downpour. If they thought themselves dirty, they knew that this water that fell from the sky would give them a new cleansing. I watched as one seagull sat on a lamppost and fluttered its wings in the misty water. He was cleansing himself, and with each flutter of his wings, he seemed to be saying "thank you." Could it be that this marvelous creature of flight knew the Almighty presence that surrounded him and was grateful for this moment that cooled and cleansed him?

Then, there was the food they ate. They did not walk up to anyone and say, "Can you spare a piece of bread or some extra bird feed." They flew with glorious speed from one location to the next, and they settled in this one spot, a parking lot. There were bread crumbs in a quiet, yet safe corner of the lot. They seemed to sound a silent cry to one another because they began to appear in abundance. Many of them were still enjoying the refreshing mist as it continued to fall. People walking by opened their umbrellas and hurried to their appointed destinations, trying to get away from the mist that was now forming into a slightly heavier rain. The seagulls were not fazed at all. They took it in, and then retreated to that corner of the parking lot for what would be considered a morning snack. This sight was very impressive to me. In those few moments that I continued to stand there, I was awestruck at how these splendid creatures wanted for nothing.

This particular passage of scripture speaks to how the birds fly in the air neither sowing nor reaping. Yet, their heavenly Father feeds them. They are literally flying without one shadow of doubt or anxiety. They are still intelligent enough to know where there is danger or where their presence is not welcomed. They do not worry about this. They fly with awe-inspiring appreciation and a gratitude for just being. I learned a lot in those brief moments of watching the seagulls fly around. I breathlessly waited as one came after the other. In my mind, I can recall seeing them at the beach, hovering around the water. It almost appears as if they were doing a dance. Their outstretched wingspan gave them a spectacular presence, one that could be frightening to the unsuspecting casual beachgoer. To a seasoned person who appreciates nature, it was like a free concert to their own dance recital. They bounced up and down, like a bobbin in a sewing machine. Their dance did not seem routine at all, yet like the seagull cleansing himself in the mist of the rain, there was gratitude in their dance. And in the midst of this performance, there was the swarm of seagulls flying about without a care in the world. They seemed locked on this one idea that "God's got me, and I am going to be all right in whatever I do. I will just spread my wings and fly." I was thoroughly impressed.

How can such magnificence be measured against a human life? Humans seem to be affected by so much more than a flock of seagulls or birds hovering at the beach. Our lives are measured in moments. Each moment that we live here has some significant meaning and value. We can either choose to embrace a moment or waste it. I chose to embrace that moment while I waited on the subway and watch those amazing creatures. I did not have to take out a notebook or videotape the moment, for it was demonstrated before me as if I were in my own private classroom. I loved this moment because, once it had passed, I went on with my day. If there was something I would have to contend with down the line, I was able to take a lesson away from that moment. A lesson where my faith was elevated just a little bit more. I did not have to worry about what was to come. And if it did come, I would deal with it in a mindset that I could still maintain some peace in my life and not stress over it. I could not literally take flight as those fine-feathered creatures did, but I could release my faith and trust in the one who was able to carry all my cares and concerns. Looking at them, I was blessed to get a glimpse into a heavenly ordered moment. To fly and not have a care in the world and be free. A life lived in faith, I knew, could give me that same freedom.

Reflective Thought

There is a train of thought that, if a person has all the money they need, they can live a worry-free life. Having an abundance of this resource will bring them more time to do all the things most people wished they could do. Time is also a valuable resource, but like anything else in life, it must be managed. It cannot be bought. You can have all the money in the world, yet you will still get a bill for something. Somehow, someway, or somewhere, having money will bring something into your life that you will have to deal with. This is an inevitable fact. There is another train of thought where an individual can elevate his level of faith and rise above anything this life presents. They can live and walk with purpose because they know God has everything under control. I may be beset with some troubles, light afflictions, and even deep heartaches, yet, when I can "spread my wings of faith and fly," I can rest in this thought: "God has got me, and I am going to be all right." You can come out of that situation, that problem, that hurt. You can be like that seagull and fly with abundant appreciation that your Heavenly Father loves you and values you more than you will ever know. He only wants the best for you. It is with that calm assurance He speaks and lets you know, "I care for you more than the birds of the field. I will provide all that you need in your greatest hour of crisis. I am here for you. Simply trust me." That is where you can abide in the "care-free life."

Chapter 2: Slow Down

A Lesson in Appreciation

"Don't hurry. Don't worry.
You're only here for a short visit.
So don't forget to stop and smell the roses."
Walter Hagen

Hollywood is not only a state of mind, but a literal place. It was my home for thirteen years, and over those years there were many challenges and lessons learned. Being a native New Yorker, I was well-equipped to handle all the madness that was Hollywood. I was used to fast, bustling crowds, strange characters, and over-the-top scenarios. I handled it with the same wisdom, savvy, and street smarts that I gained living in New York. Hollywood was also where my little furry family would originate, and I would have experiences that would teach, inspire, and cause me to grow as a man, a Christian, and a human being. Now this may seem like a lot to be contingent upon having pets, but it was my experience. It was my truth. I had two rescue cats, and it would seem like that would be enough for one person to handle. The year was 2004. I literally found Mr. Guffington, also known as Guffy, on Hollywood

Boulevard when I saw something rushing across the street in the dark. At first, thinking it was a rat, I was relegated to leaving it alone and going on my way. I wasn't about to chase after a rat. I went on and continued to the market. When I came back home, I found the most adorable black kitten hanging around my doorstep. I looked around to see if maybe he had separated from a frantic owner who was searching for him. No such luck. My property manager had a strict policy about pets. I didn't want to push the envelope and just take him in. I did bring him inside. Then, I went and got some cat food and a litter box. After all, he had nowhere to go. I did tell her, and she said that, if no one claimed him within a few days, I could keep him. His appearance was a "meant to be" moment. I felt blessed to have this precious creature come into my life the way he did.

During this time, I was working at a hotel in North Hollywood as a guest services agent. I loved my job, but it took me away from Guffy for the entire day. They say animals usually have separation anxiety, but I believe it was me who suffered from it. One of my co-workers, who knew of my love for animals, had asked me about an abandoned cat that she had found. She was beside herself with worry about what to do with this cat. This was actually how Mr. Belvedere came to be a part of my "furry family," but I will share more of his story in a subsequent chapter. Needless to say, I brought Belvedere home to be a companion for Guffy. I made sure he had all his necessary shots, and even though his initial time in our home was tepid, he eventually warmed up to us and became a vibrant part of our lives. Belvedere came from a neglected past, and I could tell by the way he responded to us. With us, he would never experience that type of treatment ever again.

I got in trouble three years later when I was at church again, and one of my fellow parishioners approached me. He was walking around the church carrying a box. His cat had just had a litter of kittens, and he desperately needed to find a home for them. He didn't want to take them to the shelter, knowing their days would be numbered if no one adopted them. I knew I should not have even looked in the box, but I did. He had about five kittens left from the original litter. There were two in the box that were absolutely beautiful. They had a grayish-black hue to their fur and the most beautiful blue eyes. In the beauty contest arena, they would be the winners, hands down. As beautiful as they were, I also noticed the one black cat in the bunch. She was considered the "runt" of the group, and it was highly probable no one would select her. Black cats, like pit bulls, had received a bad rap, and their reputation preceded them. They were considered bad luck. Oh, my friends, not this day. This "black diamond" in the rough would also steal my heart and find her place in our home. If I had taken the other two "beauties" and her, I would have named them Faith, Hope, and Charity. Faith and Hope were blessed to go to with someone else. I was left with Charity, and I am so glad I chose love. Her name and character fit her well. She was to be and still is my "Charity-girl." Ever since her arrival at our home, her name is the guiding principle I try to live by every day. Love always wins in the end.

Never in my wildest dreams had I even remotely entertained the idea of adopting a dog. I loved them immensely, but knew of the awesome responsibility it took to raise and care for them. I was known as the "cat man," and I gladly wore the title. By this time, I had secured another position, and we had moved into a much bigger place. I was happy that my three felines had adjusted and were getting along. Of course, Guffy started to look at me like I was crazy, as if to say, "if this man brings one more animal in this house, I'm walking. I know where the front door is, and I can open it, too! Keep playing with me." (And he really did know how to open the door!) This attitude went on for several months, but we soon got back to normal. Of course, I had to tempt the waters one more time when I came upon a private adoption fair. I saw the most beautiful puppies who were full of life with looks of hope in their eyes. I told myself, "Stay away from those puppies, Hartford, because you know what is going to happen." Did I listen? No. I just had to stop by and pet a few of them and maybe hold one or two. During this time, I was able to speak to the young lady who represented the rescue shelter. She told me they were running out of space and needed to find homes for these precious pups soon. I just so happened to catch the attention of one dog in particular. She had the most beautiful coat and incredible brown eyes. She was a Maltese-terrier mix with a white coat that was so befitting of her. I looked at her. She looked at me. I picked her up. She licked my ear. The young lady, whose name was Rachel, told me her name was Ginger. I kept looking into those eyes. I tried to explain to Ginger (in my own Dr. Doolittle-ish way) that I had three cats, and there was no more room at the inn (literally). She nuzzled up to me and wagged that tail. Then a word I was quite familiar with came up — *foster*. I, then, spoke with Rachel about fostering one of the pups (namely the one that was in my arms). I wanted to help them as they seemed desperate to find homes, even if it meant a "foster home" for these beautiful canines. I dared not look at the others because then I would have an army following me back to my house. Of course, one resident was threatening to move out. Mr. Guffington had his bag and catnip ready to go. Dare I tempt the waters? How would I manage my schedule if I brought this beautiful creature home? I looked into those brown eyes again, and then it happened. Ginger licked my ears. I was hooked and knew, from that moment, she was going to be my dog. I started the initial paperwork with Rachel and her team and said this was only going to be a trial period. Who did I think I was kidding? In about three weeks, I was writing the check to cover all the adoption fees. I knew there would be some tension when I brought her home. The chief cat was not feeling her. I prayed about keeping her and also prayed for there not to be an upheaval in the Hough household. In the end, peace won out the day. Belvedere was an absolute gem and warmed up to Ginger right away. Charity was happy that another female had entered the domicile. Yes, things balanced out, and I was grateful for those moments. There was still another beautiful lesson I was to learn. It would come about from a simple walk with Ginger.

Ginger had been living with me for four months. It was an interesting adjustment watching her get used to my cats as she did. She never felt threatened or intimidated by them. Many who knew me were quite aware that I had three cats who made up my world, Mr. Belvedere, and Mr. Guffington (Guffy), and Charity. It was a fascinating dynamic to watch these three interact. Ginger would stay on the couch and just wait for me to come home from work. Belvedere was always trying to be hospitable and friendly. He was still very shy, but he had come out of his shell in recent years, and it was nice to see more of his personality. Guffy could care less about either one (or so I thought). For you see, Guffy was my "sentry guard." No matter what happened in our household, I knew this cat would stand by me. He never let the emotions rattle him. As he grew older and wiser, this was what I came to love about him even more. He wasn't even bothered when Ginger and I went on our daily walks twice a day. It was as if he almost told Ginger, "You make sure you bring him back because it's almost time to eat and my litter box needs cleaning." In her own unique way, the wag of her tail said she understood and would comply.

It was a typical day for our walk. Ginger had readied herself because she knew this was "our time," and she looked forward to it, as did I. We had a basic routine that we covered every day for our walk, and rarely did we stray from it. On this particular day, I found myself hurrying because I was tired and just wanted to go home and rest. I did want to allow Ginger her space of about forty-five minutes to an hour to get her walk on, and to exercise and play with the other neighborhood dogs. She loved that time. I could see it in her face, and her body language told me that she simply wanted to take her time. I, on the other hand, wanted to get through it and get back to the house. Daddy had worked all day, and he wanted to go home, eat, and relax for the evening, but Ginger was not having it.

She did not put up a fuss or aggressively fight against me, but she did do something that was unusual, and I had to take notice. She began walking really slow, smelling every bush, flower, and tree that was along our route. We lived in Hollywood, so there were lots of trees and bushes. I marveled at how she enjoyed the moment of it all and how it was purposefully done. Because dogs cannot communicate like humans, we have to learn to read body language from them and pay attention to the signals they give us. It is so easy to ignore these signals when we are caught up in our own world and they are just viewed as animals out on a walk.

In her body language to me, she was basically saying, "Slow down, my human friend. I know you love me, as I do you. Let's enjoy this moment. Why are we rushing back to the house? The cats will be fine; you know how independent they are. Look at nature and all these beautiful flowers. If you keep rushing, you will miss it." It was in that moment that the realization of why she had slowed down struck me. It wasn't because she was ill or being obstinate. She was trying to tell me to appreciate the walk and all that we were encountering. It was good for both of us. It was good for our health, and it bonded us closer as a human to his animal companion. I will always value that day and remember the lesson that my dog taught me in "learning to slow down and smell the roses."

Reflective Thought

Our lives are but a vapor. We are only here but for a short time, and we must make the most of the time that God has allowed us. We must appreciate and value those things that are important — our family, friends, faith, and community. God is not limited by time and space. He is not measured in hours, minutes, and seconds. What we think of as an exorbitant amount of time does not even measure up to God. He is eternal. Yet, in this human experience, our lives are measured in moments. God, being omniscient, is in every moment of our lives. These moments are meant to teach us something. When you take that time to "stop and smell the roses," you are acknowledging that everything has worth, and you regard those things with gratitude. From a simple flower to a fully constructed skyscraper, all have a place in this world and should be regarded for their value and contribution. Never take anything for granted because it can truly be here today and gone tomorrow.

Chapter 3: Patience

A Lesson in Patience

"Waiting is a sign of true love and patience. Anyone can say I love you, but not everyone can wait and prove it's true."
Unknown

How many times a day is our patience tested? From the kids acting up at the start of the day to the frustration that grows from sitting in traffic or the myriad of problems that come up in between. Patience is that part of our character that seems to need the most development over our lifetime. The tests and challenges that try our patience come in many forms. It usually starts off with small tests that we seemingly can brush off as no big deal. After all, the client was just ten minutes late for the meeting. There is no need to stress and pull our hair out over that. We figure there might have been traffic or some other delay. It especially calms our stress level when the person calls and says they are running late. We can breathe a small sigh, relax, and just wait for the client to arrive. After all, you know they are coming. Take that test up a few notches, and a whole new scenario is created.

You are on your way to work. You leave your house in enough time to drive to the station, park, and then board your train.

Then that dreaded announcement comes, "Ladies and gentlemen, we are experiencing a fifteen to twenty-minute delay on all trains heading into the city. We apologize for the inconvenience." "Apology not accepted. You gave us that same announcement yesterday and caused me to be late for my appointment." With some mutterings under your breath, you have to exercise patience somehow. You know you are not going to go back and drive into the city. The thought of morning traffic makes you crazy. You bide your time, and hopefully the delay will be rectified soon. The delays and the crowds are getting on everyone's last nerve. The crowd is swelling as more people file into the station. You know the trains will be more crowded than ever. Hence, even more delays. This is only the beginning of your patience being tested and escalating to a whole new level.

When you finally arrive in the city, it is only to find out there is a power outage in the area where you work. You make it to your building, but you are redirected to wait outside until you hear from someone from your department. You figure you can go get some coffee, only to find they have no power as well, and your patience is tried once again. Not only are you late in getting to work. Now you may not be able to work. Some may consider this a great thing. Others, not so. You are working on a project that has to be completed by the end of the week. These interruptions are causing more time to be lost. Then, you receive a call saying the deadline has been moved up. They do not want to hear about traffic or train delays. They want the report finished and in their office in two days! Ouch! Now you may feel you are just about to lose it.

Can patience be quelled as you abide there awaiting a positive outcome? Consider another figure in this scenario that you probably never thought about. How would they view this situation? If you are blessed to own a dog, you may not realize that this can be a source of a very teachable moment, while also helping you understand what patience really is. Your dog sits at home all day after you leave. He is not fettered by the same issues that you may experience on a daily basis, yet he waits. All he knows is that you go out that door and you are gone for a long period of time. "Where is he going?" "Why does he leave for such a long period? I want him to stay with me all day, but he leaves." Your faithful canine companion still loves you regardless of how long you are gone. And with an amazing burst of energy, he will greet you when you come through that door. He must bide his heart in patience and wait for you.

As he waits, there will probably be long periods of sleep and naps throughout the day. Ever alert, he listens for any sound that comes to his attention. Whether it be a car passing by the house or the neighbor's dog barking relentlessly, your faithful companion is listening out for you to come through that door. Periodically, he may shift locations in the house, all the while keeping a vigil for you. You have given him enough food and water to sustain him throughout the day. He knows how much you care for him. You even leave the air conditioner on, so the house is nice and cool, even when the temperature is escalating outside. He only feels the cool and comfort of being in the place you have made his home. He has no idea what is going on throughout the course of your day. All he knows is to love you and be there when you come home.

What is patience? It is the capacity to accept or tolerate delay, trouble, or suffering without getting angry or upset. Our animal companions exercise an incredible capacity to accept these long delays and not get ruffled. What an amazing depth of character we as humans would possess if we practiced this in our daily lives. We, too, possess the capacity to accept or tolerate delay and trouble. We simply choose not to exercise it. Herein is the lesson learned from our animal companion. He is experiencing a long day without you being there. He has no one to play with. No one to take him outside and exercise. And the latter part of that definition on patience is where the lesson truly hits home. "They accept or tolerate without getting upset or angry." Wow! When you finally do come through that door, you are greeted by a wagging tail and an overly expressive animal that has loved you all along. His love for you never wavered. He doesn't care how long it took for you to come back home. All he knows it that you are there now, and he can share in making your day (with all its madness) subside with furry affection, kisses of love, and the consolation that you are both together again.

Reflective Thought

Life gives us so many challenges, and sometimes, we simply want to ignore them and look away. If we didn't have to deal with them, we probably would feel we were better off. Yet they keep coming. Our characters will be a lifetime project in development. There are some of us who have been through so much in our lifetimes that we have nothing else to do but wait. We are not just waiting to be waiting. We know the outcome of whatever the problem is will work itself out. When we lose patience, we become frustrated with ourselves and with others. Often, this can be projected with a bad attitude or angry temperament. We know this is not how we want to live our lives. We are better than that. Our four-legged companions know of the virtue of patience all too well. They exercise it every day, all the time. They have, just as humans, an amazing capacity to withstand long delays or trouble. Part of their purpose is to be here for us. If you are waiting over two hours for a bus to arrive, they don't care as long as you are there with them, watching and protecting them. They are also there for you, providing you forever companionship and devotion, knowing that, if you two can wait this out together, you will both be all right.

Chapter 4: Undying Devotion

A Lesson in True Devotion

"So if I ever get my hand on a dollar again, I'm gonna hold on to
it 'til them eagles grin
Nobody knows you, when you down and out
In my pocket not one penny, and my friends I haven't any."
From "Nobody Knows You When You're Down and Out" by
Jimmy Cox

It was a heart-wrenching scene of loneliness and despair. She sat on the sidewalk corner with her bare essentials and a glimmer of hope that maybe someone would spare her some change or a bite to eat. I had seen her there many times before. Depending on the nature of the elements, she would either be visible or absent from my sight. I did not desperately seek her out. She was someone I saw on my way to work in the morning. I would often see her as she readied herself for the throngs of people that would be coming through the area. People going to work, school, or running errands. They came from all walks of life — rich, middle-class, working class, young, old, black, white, Asian, and Latino. They exited the buses or or ascended the subway stairs and began their rushed journeys to their points of destination. In the midst of all this was the woman who had no one. She had her cardboard placards ready as she saw the people coming, hoping they would spare some change or a morsel of food. She took a moment to slightly tidy her area up as the people were coming. She felt, if she could make some impression on them, they would pity her and offer assistance. There was also something else that struck me as I watched this woman. When she sat down, there lay on her lap a faithful, devoted canine. Regardless of the situation, he was unmoved as his place of care and loyalty lay there with this woman.

It could have been a most beautiful sight, but it was not. I had just disembarked from the train, and thousands of people swarmed the downtown area of San Francisco. Many were so focused on getting to their destination that they paid her no attention. Others tuned out the noise and obvious surroundings with their headsets and earplugs. It was almost as if they purposely did not want to be bothered. She was just another transient on the street. Why should she be their concern? After all, she would simply move to another location and try to bum something from another group of people. People were already disillusioned with the homeless crisis. If they could spare some change, they would. If not, no big deal. Add to this image a poor, defenseless dog, and then what did you have?

How could I not stop and say something? Not just because of the dog, but this was another human being who should not be living like this. I would not ask why she was out there. I was awestruck by her loyal companion's devotion to her. She called his name and he responded. He looked with longing eyes to do whatever he could to serve her and make her day. I had just obtained my own breakfast sandwich and could not just walk by her and not offer some help. As she gladly received the food, I sensed a lightness in her voice when she spoke of her animal companion.

She was all too happy to share a portion of her food with him. And he was happy to receive it. To the naked eye, this could be viewed as a sad situation, but I saw this as something more. In my heart, I was challenged to do something to try to help this woman in her plight. I believe that is the Christ in me. This single situation reminded me of when Jesus saw the multitude and was moved with compassion to help them.

I had to focus in on the dog for a moment. He did not care that his situation was one of despair. He wasn't aware of life's problems. All he knew was to stand by his human companion and never leave her side. If someone remotely seemed to threaten her or their environment as they had come to know it, he would growl with protective warning. His devotion to her was so evident to me. I stood there and observed for a few moments more. The devotion of this pitiful creature was becoming a most beautiful moment to me as a human. How can we get to a place where we look beyond our own problems, no matter how great or small, and yet remain devoted to another person or cause? It becomes a selfless act when you forget about your concerns and focus on another individual. He knew he was cared for and loved and remained steadfast by his human companion. I had, at times, frowned upon these types of scenarios. As of late, my heart had lightened to look a little deeper at the situation. It was not my place to judge or belittle her. I could help where I could. She had the best of the best, even in her plight of despair. She had this wonderful creature unmoved by the cares of life standing by her side.

Her name was Karen. She had an ebullient spirit about her and was always most willing to speak to anyone. The interesting thing about Karen was that she offered more of a listening ear to other people than it seemed they had for her. She was most open to hear what other people had to say, and though she could not offer help to their situation, she could infuse some of her life experiences into the conversation. I imagine Karen had had a decent life before she ended up here. Just from talking with her, I knew she was a woman who had been educated and experienced life on her terms. She had just made some poor choices. I had once heard someone say, "We are where we are today because of a choice we made yesterday." I am sure Karen wanted better for her life. She was just getting through the day the best way she knew how. She did stay at a local shelter, but they had to leave every morning and were only able to return at night. Karen was just grateful her dog was able to be with her. The dog's name was Mandarin.

On another occasion, I had the opportunity to talk a bit more with Karen about her situation. She had faced some pretty hard times. For she and her dog, it was about survival. It is here that my heart bleeds for those persons in these situations. I may not be able to help everyone, but if in some small way, I can make a difference, thank God. I was very glad she had the company of Mandarin. Having this responsibility made her more astute in her situation. She knew her limitations, but was determined to overcome them and get back to the place she once knew and regarded as normal for her life. I gave her a few dollars and offered to buy some food for Mandarin, a healthy looking pit-bull mixed with shepherd. He was also grateful for any treats and goodies that came his way. I looked into those eyes, and I knew this dog would stay with Karen come hell or high water. He was devoted to her. It was in those times that I wished I could do something special for her animal companion like take him for a walk, or to a doggie park, or for a run along the beach. He only knew of the love and care he received from his owner. He, and all pets in general, didn't understand homelessness. Being down and out, as I have stated before does not deter animals, for all animals respond to love. If they know love, they feel safe, warm, and protected.

Reflective Thought

What is undying devotion? It is that love, loyalty, and enthusiasm for another person. Undying simply means "lasting forever." It is this "permanent" devotion that makes the person who is in the worst of a situation feel better. I used to be very hard on persons who were transient and had dogs or cats. How can they take care of this poor animal when they can barely take care of themselves? After talking with Karen, I had some more insight into the situation, and it caused me to reflect. Some of these animals had been with them long before they ended up where they did. In the loss of property and possessions, their furry companions were some of the most precious things that stayed with them. If they had better options on the care of their animals, they would have chosen it for them. Unfortunately, these options were few and far between. The undying devotion of this creature was something of a "healing balm" for them. As most pet parents do, we refer to our fur babies as "our children." Just because we go through a hard time, we do not cast away our beloved creatures. Such was the case for Karen and Mandarin. His undying devotion to her gave her hope. When people stopped and talked with her and listened, this elevated her hope and faith just a little higher. I was glad I made her acquaintance, and I only wished the best for her. If help or other resources became available, I would extend them to her. As long as they are alive, they can have hope. I would only pray that no one would ever try to eradicate that hope from her.

Chapter 5: Hope Against All Odds

A Lesson in Hope

"To love means loving the unlovable. To forgive means pardoning the unpardonable. Faith means believing the unbelievable. Hope means hoping when everything seems hopeless."
Gilbert K. Chesterton

When we wake up in the morning, we have no idea what will be the outcome of the day. It can turn out to be a wonderful, fun-filled day, full of excitement and adventure. It can also take a bad turn and go in a not so favorable direction. Whatever the outcome, we have to continue to keep hope in our hearts and not diminish its powerful working. Hope is a wonderful quality to possess. It brings forth expectation, an expectation for good things to happen. Expecting the day to turn out the way you had wanted it to. Expecting that long-awaited phone call or visit. Hope burns in us like an eternal flame that will not be quenched. It is an ever-going furnace that continues to draw heat from its hearth and motivates us to believe in something greater than ourselves. It is that kind of hope that has the expectation that what you are working toward will eventually come to an end and all things in your life will be fulfilled. Hope drives us to go to those unexpected places where we can see the top of the mountain. The mission will not be finished until we saw off the top of the mountain. Hope gives us sheer will. It is that "push" behind you that says, "move forward because it will be all right."

It was a routine Saturday for me. We had just relocated to the Bay Area and were comfortably settling in to our new surroundings. I had become familiar with the area and was very happy to find a local branch of Petco nearby. It was the one place where I had to be careful because I could spend a cool fortune on my animals, spoiling them with toys, treats, and other services. On this particular day, I needed to get some flea medication for Charity. I looked through the many choices and even asked the clerk's opinion, which was a decision I would later regret. She recommended a medication that was designed for canines, and unwittingly felt, because the ingredients were similar, it would be okay for cats. It was here that I must say, "Trust your first voice." I always believe this is when God is speaking to your heart. I didn't see the girl as doing this on purpose to hurt my cat. She just did not know.

I administered the medication to Charity when I returned home and began preparing for Sunday, as my church was having its services outside in the park the next day. I had also volunteered to help out, though I was a new member. Later that evening, I began to hear a yelping sound coming from another area of the apartment. I looked at Ginger and saw that she was okay. I still couldn't figure out where this sound was coming from. I then noticed it was Charity, and she was having what appeared to be "fits of a seizure." My heart panicked because Charity was always healthy and fit. I picked her up to see what was wrong, and she went into a full-out seizure. Thank God there was a twenty-four-hour emergency vet care near where I lived. I called them and explained the situation, and they instructed me to bring her in. My heart was racing because I had seen Charity's brother go through a similar crisis right before he passed. "This cannot be happening again. Not to my Charity-girl. I can't lose her now." In my frazzled state, I prayed. I set my heart to hope. Hope being "a feeling of expectation for a certain thing to happen." I gave the situation and Charity to God.

It is here when our faith is challenged in these most critical moments that we must release the situation to God. We do have a tendency to hold on to it, and this can make us even more harried as the situation continues to develop. I know what an emotional person I am, and sometimes, my emotions do get the better of me. We must also place this in God's hands as well. A simple prayer of "God, please keep my heart and mind, for you know this situation better than I do. I trust you to handle it." Sometimes this may seem like small consolation when the matter is right in your face. I would have never thought myself to be in this position at this hour of the morning. I wanted to call some of my friends, but it was 2:30 a.m. And what would I say? There was nothing to do but yield to the only option I knew (and had at that moment). Faith caused me to turn my face to the wall.

After taking her to the emergency room at the veterinary hospital, I sat in that room and cried my eyes out. The doctors rushed to stabilize her and took her into emergency. My beloved Ginger, who also knew something was wrong, was right there with me. Though I was crying endlessly, she sat in my lap and comforted me, as if to say, "She is going to be all right. Keep that hope in your heart." I did. I knew the Creator of Life had this situation in His hands, and I simply had to trust Him. Looking at Ginger always gave me a sense of calm. Just the fact that she was there was comforting enough. Plus, it was an animal hospital, and there was no way they were going to keep her from her "best bud" in this hour of crisis. I laid my hand on Ginger's head and ceased my tears. I had to do exactly what Ginger would've been saying to me — "Keep hope in your heart."

A few hours later, the doctor came out with a good report. They had stabilized her and told me I could take her home. She had had a bad reaction to the flea medicine, and it almost taken her out. My heart was so relieved when I was able to see my precious Charity and how my hope had come to its fruition. She was going to be okay. My hope set in motion a feeling of expectation. I could not allow my emotions to run rampant, but rest in the fact that what I had prayed for, and hoped in God, would come to pass. Hope, being the first cousin of faith, is all God asks of us. He just asks us to trust Him, in EVERY situation. Faith pleases Him. It also causes His hands to do what no human could — move a near-death situation to life and restore health for a precious, vibrant animal. To this day, Charity has been good and as healthy ever since.

Reflective Thought

What do you do in what seems like a hopeless situation? Losing hope means losing that expectation for a good outcome. Another way of putting it is that you have given up. The dark clouds seem to weigh you down, and you can barely see a ray of light (or that glimmer of hope). Trust me, IT IS THERE. We often hope for so many things. A new job, a new car, or even a new relationship. Sometimes hope can come to us in smaller situations and teach us that the feeling is valid and that we must not lose it. When a bad situation comes upon us, many tend to do what I do, panic. Fear so often sets in. After all, we are human. Once we calm ourselves and allow that which we believe to take over, things do change. Hope motivates us to believe a little further and a whole lot stronger. It causes us not to panic, as we may, but trust. My beloved cat could have lost her life that day. I exercised HOPE against all the odds (poor advice, bad reactions to medicine, and former tragedies), and allowed that feeling of expectation for a good outcome. God was faithful to provide that.

Ms. Charity

Chapter 6: Unique Bonds of Friendship

A Lesson in Friendship

"Do I not destroy my enemies when I make them my friends?"
Abraham Lincoln

In nature, the natural enemy of the mongoose is the snake. In particular, the cobra. A mongoose, because of its size, possesses speed and agility. The snake, on the other hand, possesses a deadly venom. If you have ever been privileged to observe a zoology lab and see these two natural enemies, it would prove to be most enlightening. For you see, when the mongoose sees the snake, there is a relentless activity between the two, and the desire to seemingly fight is all they want to achieve. The mongoose is very well stirred up by the presence of the snake and lets out shrieking cries. These would almost seem like fits of anger at the sight of his opponent. The snake, slithering in its confinement, lets out bone-chilling hisses that prove he is a worthy opponent and not afraid. Should these two ever come in contact with each other, their meeting would set the stage for an epic battle.

The mongoose literally hates the snake. Mongeese are skilled hunters with an exceptionally keen sense of sight, smell and hearing. Many animals are caught unaware of a snake's presence because it moves ever so quickly across the surface and can be very quiet and unnoticeable. This is how many humans are bitten by snakes because we are not often aware of their presence and they catch us off guard. Mongeese are not so easily taken. They can sense the presence of a snake that are several feet away, and automatically the mongoose goes into attack mode. The snake may think he is upon his prey, but his prey is more than ready for a showdown.

In human life, there have been people who really hate each other. The dictionary defines hatred as "intense dislike or ill will." The feeling of hatred can come from many different factors. There can be general dislike for another person or their presence, dislike for their clothing, economic status, familial relations, or even their intellect. Hatred is not something that comes naturally. We do not just go around hating other people. It is an emotion that manifests itself through a learned behavior. You may not like another person, but hatred is something that is built up over time. The awful part about hatred is that you carry ill will toward another human being. This means you wish for their demise. You hate them so much you wish them bodily harm or the expiration of their life. Hatred is one of those emotions with which we must be very careful. We should never be so filled with this emotion that we would want that for another human life. It is understandable to be angry with another person. Anger can be managed and controlled. Hatred goes deeper.

It has also been said of two other animals that they have a natural animosity toward one another and that their being in each other's presence can cause quite a furor. Most of us have heard the term: "They were fighting like cats and dogs." Well, this term derived from somewhere and never has a statement been more unfounded in error. Cats and dogs have completely opposite personalities. Cats are far more independent when it comes to their basic grooming and hygiene, survival tactics, and appeasing nature in dealing with their surrounding environment. Some cats are extremely affectionate, while other breeds are more standoffish. All cats genuinely respond to love and care, but still take the independent road when doing things on their own. Dogs are far more dependent on humans. From being puppies to adults, they generally take to a human and carry that seal throughout their lifetimes. I believe this is where that natural animosity between the two animals originates. One breed is independent, and the other, not so much. When this is encroached upon by one of the other species, it sets a bad tone. To see a dog and a cat who really dislike each other is very disturbing. Unlike the mongoose and the snake, their predatory nature is not to seek each other out and engage in a fight. Normally, they just ignore each other until they are brought together.

The interesting dynamic is that these two creatures possess an ability to become the very best of friends. A dog does have a predatory nature like his older, more carnivorous ancestor, the wolf. Their instinct would be to hunt down a cat, but not always. For these two creatures, who both can be wonderfully domesticated, share a common trait with humans — companionship. I have witnessed firsthand the socialization process of these two. Dogs, who can exude a wide range of emotions, can become lonely. When we leave our beloved canines alone all day, they do indeed miss us. In the presence of another living creature, they find some sense of solace, as if to say, "I am not alone here. There is another living being in this place with me." In the beginning, the two may present themselves to be hostile enemies. As time moves on, they slowly develop a bond that unites them. Watching this unfold is really a beautiful transformation.

On a personal take, I have watched this beautiful act take place between my dog Ginger and my cat Charity. After the death of her brothers, Charity did stay to herself. She would nuzzle up with me when I came home, but then retreat to her elevated cat condo. She rarely interacted with Ginger, who was always waiting for me with such devotion and steadfast behavior. In time, I watched these two come out of their shells and become very close to each other. It was in my absence during the day that they realized they could be there for each other. They were never really left alone. Their bond became so strong that now Ginger hates to be separated from her feline buddy. It warms my heart as I watch the closeness of these two.

As humans, we may declare someone to be our enemy. There may even be a level of animosity and tension. Yet, when we reach out to another living soul to relate and co-exist, we find that the walls that surrounded us as enemies slowly begins to break down. Take for example the hardcore neighbor. He/she may not like living next door to you for some ridiculous reason, like you entertain too many people all the time. As you live next door, you come to realize that the you must co-exist with this person somehow. Walls can be slowly broken down by a smile. A kind gesture. A gracious attitude. Every human being, no matter how cold-hearted they may seem, can experience kindness and love on some level, a level that touches the heart. When that neighbor realizes that what kept you apart and unkind to each other is really small potatoes in the grand scheme of things, he/she can begin to have a change of heart. I believe this is where God's working on the heart makes all the difference. And when God works on the human heart, there really can be a transformation of a life.

Reflective Thought

It has been said that "opposites attract and likes repel." There may be some degree of truth in this, but not necessarily when it comes to various species. You can have two totally different individuals with absolutely nothing in common. Yet, once they communicate with each other, they will soon find out that the differences between them are more common than they thought. It is those differences that can bring them closer together once walls and barriers have been broken down to reach a common ground, as in the case of the two neighbors who may not like each other and feel they have nothing in common. Just the fact that you live in the same neighborhood is a common trait between the two. You will have to deal with neighborhood issues and try to resolve them as only neighbors can. You may shop at the same supermarket or even attend the same place of worship. Humans, like animals, may have differences between them. When they recognize those differences, and learn to accept each other as they are, even the walls of tension and hatred can be broken down to form a friendship. Both parties realize the need for common socialization, and something as simple as a "good morning" or "have a nice day" can be the catalyst that breaks things down and brings forth mutual respect and admiration.

Chapter 7: Learning to Say Goodbye

A Lesson on Death and Dying

"The reality is that you will grieve forever. You will not 'get over' the loss of a loved one; you will learn to live with it. You will heal and you will rebuild yourself around the loss you have suffered. You will be whole again but you will never be the same. Nor should you be the same nor would you want to."
Elisabeth Kubler-Ross

Death is never an easy subject to talk about. I have known this inevitable fact all my life. I remember the first time I encountered death. Mama McBride took me out with her shopping. I was all of five years old, but I remember the day as if it were yesterday. She went about her errands and had me in tow. I didn't care where we went; I was just happy to be out with Mama. It was a warm, spring day. Most of her errands took place in the neighborhood, so I was very familiar with all the buildings, stores, and schools that I saw. At one point, we got on a bus and headed downtown. It was not too far. We got off the bus, and she went about her tasks. I remember being a little bit of a nuisance. Every so often, she would have to shrug my arm to get me to cooperate and get back in line with her command. Mama did not play when it came to discipline and obedience.

After we boarded the bus and were heading down Fulton Street, back home, I looked out and saw the familiar lining of apartment buildings, stores, and other neighborhood points of interest. We disembarked from the bus, and Mama and I walked toward another building I was not familiar with. It was a brick building with a short awning in the front. It almost resembled a small church. I knew it was not as big as the church we attended on Sunday mornings. There were stained glass windows and very large brown doors with oversized door handles. Everything looked big to me. After all, I was only five. The building was nestled between two other buildings that were obvious residential units. The neighborhood was bustling with an afternoon crowd as Mama and I navigated our way to the doors of this unusual, unfamiliar building. To most children, there would be a sense of wonder and amazement when entering something new. I was not prepared for what was beyond those large brown doors.

Once inside, the entire atmosphere changed. The mood became very quiet and somber. There was an unusual smell in the air. Initially I would say it was the smell of the flowers that seemingly adorned the entire room. I remember those smells. The roses were fragrant. The tulips were beautifully arranged in a basket that stood on a stand. There was no music or any other sound except that of our own voices. Mama was greeted by a very tall man wearing a black suit. They chatted for a moment. I watched them both very carefully, wondering what they were preparing me to see. After she finished talking, she grabbed my hand, and we entered another room. This room was even more different than the first. I noticed rows of chairs that looked like the ones that were in our fellowship hall at church. They were simple wooden chairs with red plush cushioning on the backs and seats. The room was even darker and was lit by several flickering lights that created an almost scary effect. In the middle of this was a large box. I looked beyond Mama's figure and noticed that there was something unusual about this box. There was someone in it! I wasn't scared because Mama never let go of my hand, and fear had no place here. I watched Mama as her expression became very sad. As most inquisitive children do, I bombarded her with questions. "Mama, who is that?" "What is she doing in that box?" "Why is she not moving?" "Mama, what's wrong?" She explained to me, and I remember it to this day, that the woman in the box was a friend of hers from church. She had died, and she was now taking her rest. She was asleep, but that one day, she was going to get up and be with the Lord. Our pastor had talked about the Lord and how, when people die, they go to live with Him forever. I figured that this was where Mama's friend was. I knew her friend was asleep, and I told Mama, "We better leave now and not wake her up." Mama had a few more moments with her friend, and then we took our leave. This was my introduction to death. It was a presence that I remember from the first time, and know all too well to this day.

Death can be considered an unwelcomed visitor. When death comes, it usually takes something or someone away. As a child, I just figured death put them to sleep, but they would wake up again, someday. I also noticed that, when death came, people became very sad. They would cry a lot and, sometimes, have terrible outbursts of anger. Death had an effect on people. I also noticed this same effect when it came to losing a beloved pet. Losing friends and family to death is never easy. Sometimes, you wrestle with this loss for months, even years. The hardest part of this loss is having to say goodbye. How do you do it?

Belvedere was my beloved tabby whom I had rescued from an impoverished situation through a co-worker. I never knew Belvedere's real age. He had to have been older than I imagined. I was, nonetheless, very happy to welcome him into my home and into my life. I already had Mr. Guffington, and he had transitioned very nicely into our lives. He also came to know Ginger and Charity as his friendly animal companions when I was away. I never thought about the day when he might have to leave us. Belvedere responded to love and affection in such a marvelous way that I believe it healed his little soul. He knew, in our presence, there was kindness, compassion, and undying love.

That fateful day came seven years after Belvedere came to live with us. He never really experienced any major health problems. If he did, I addressed them with the vet, and it was resolved. Things went on as usual. One day, I noticed he was using the bathroom quite a lot. It was far more unusual than his regular relief sessions. I sensed there was a problem, and I prayed that it would go away. The situation only grew worse for him. I dare not see my precious Belvedere suffer, so I took him back to the vet. We discovered he had an infection in his urinary tract. It was pretty serious because they had to keep him overnight. He stayed there, was treated, and was released. Even upon his return home, I knew there was still something wrong, and my heart feared that the inevitable was coming. I watched him over the next few days as his pace became slower and slower. He was having trouble walking, and it seemed to be in a lot of pain. "Not my Belvedere. I do not want to lose him this way." All I know is that when he slowly walked around the house, it hurt my heart that much more to watch him. I had to mentally prepare myself for what I knew was coming.

On the Saturday before he was about to make his transition, my neighbor came by. I took him outside, carrying him in my arms. He had lost so much weight, and the lightness of his body tore me down that much more. He was slipping away. He liked the sunshine and the attention my neighbor was showing him. I wanted that moment with him to last forever, but it did not. The next day, I was scheduled to be at church to oversee the weekly fellowship. I had made some desserts, and my friend came by to take me to church. I stood at her car and broke down. I could not leave him this way. I could not leave my precious "Poo-Boo." I had to forfeit going to church. I gave her my desserts and said I would call her later. I sat with him the entire time, humming songs and talking with him as if he were not going anywhere. Guffy sat and watched as his buddy slowly slipped away. In his typical fashion, he showed no emotion, just stood guard and watched him. Ginger sat by me the entire time. She clung to me as if she knew something was happening, and she would not leave my side. I will always appreciate her for that. Charity played "Ms. Standoffish." She sat on her perched cat condo and watched. She knew.

The hours withered away as Belvedere's breathing became slow and heavy. I sat by him and stroked his golden fur. I hoped for the best, but prepared myself for what was coming. I took him in my arms and held him. I cried because I did not want to lose my boy. Guffington's pal. Charity's go-to companion. Ginger's hospitable mate. He had become the heart of our little family, and he was leaving us. At 2:01 pm on Sunday, October 16, 2011, Belvedere took his last breath in my arms. Death had come once again. I could not fight it, but when it came, I had a sense of peace with this loss. He was not suffering anymore. I wept openly as each of my animals knew, in that moment, he was gone.

I realized that, during this whole process, I was already preparing myself to say goodbye. As I stated before, I knew death all too well. It was not so welcome, but its assignment came to claim another precious life. I saw that, once again, death was a part of life. So many times before, this truth had come back to me. I cried. Guffy withdrew himself for a while. Charity and Ginger became my rocks of strength. They all reminded me that, in the midst of what just happened, our lives had to go on. Ginger, only three years old at the time, always made sure we still took our daily walks. In learning to say goodbye, you come to realize it is a process over time, not just in the moment. In the weeks that followed, I found cathartic ways to deal with my grief. I looked at pictures. I spoke with friends. I availed myself to be busy and keep my mind going. In our own ways, we all said our goodbyes, yet the memory of this precious and beloved cat lives in our hearts forever.

In processing the death of a pet, we can see where the five stages of death are readily applied to each and every individual situation. The first stage of *denial* comes because we simply cannot believe that our beloved pet is gone. Even in the act of putting a pet down, we still don't want to believe the vet when they come out and tell us our furry companion is gone. Something grips us and shakes us to the core in open denial. When we return home, we still believe we are going to see them come around the corner and greet us. We are then confronted with *anger*. We are angry at God and ourselves for letting something like this happen. We want to believe God gave us this animal to love and care for, yet now they are being taken away. We are angry with ourselves because we feel like we let our animal companion down. We failed them. Now they are gone. *Bargaining* comes when we feel like we can make a deal over what has happened. Here again, we bargain with God, ourselves, and even others. We want to try to make good on a deal that, if we do something, there will be a fair exchange for us in the end. For example, we bargain to do better if we get another pet. We soon forget how good we were to our former pet, and we now feel that the latter will even out for us. If these things don't pan out, we find ourselves slipping into depression. *Depression* can take an awful toll on us, physically and emotionally. It is always present now because our companion animal is no longer there. It is a constant reminder to us, and that sends us into a semi- or full-depressive state. In depression, we often stop doing what we know is right for us to do, and stay away from it. It causes us great pain, and can literally begin to control our lives. It is here that we must seek out help. Talk to a friend. Seek grief counseling. Join a support group of others who have lost their pets. Talk it through until you are in a better place. Realizing you are not alone in what has befallen you can allow you to face the last stage of death, *acceptance*. When you have reached this phase, you have come to a place of peace within yourself over the loss of your beloved pet. You accept the facts that surrounded their passing, especially if they were older and dealing with health issues (e.g. arthritis, blindness). You accept that they were not meant to suffer like that, and their passing, though it was hard, gives you comfort that they are no longer suffering or in pain. They are free.

For me, I have always turned to my faith immediately to get me through the process of losing a pet. I have relied on God to sustain my mind and my health as I deal with the coming days after I have lost them. As mentioned before, it was also the presence of my current animals as a reminder that life has to go on. We cannot wallow in this state too long. Life is still for living. If you are blessed to have another animal companion after the loss of one, this is a sweet reminder.

Reflective Thought

Death is a part of life that we must all deal with at some time or another. It is a time of loss that you can never really prepare for. In the process of death and dying, you never want to see another individual suffer, whether it be of cancer, an aneurysm, or some other terminal disease, for these all have an effect on the person or persons that are left behind. This is also true in the loss of a beloved pet. We consider them to be members of our family. So, when they pass, there is indeed a "death in the family." You can be prepared for this type of loss. There comes a point when you have to accept the reality of what is happening. There are indeed five stages to the process of death. Each person must go through each phase and deal with it on their own terms. Always remember that when this phase of a person's life is over, life does, indeed, go on. Losing a pet presents the same position. You can immerse yourself in grief, or you can choose to treasure the love and memories, and move forward. Life will always present painful, hard situations, but we can face the pain and choose to move on because beyond the pain there is healing and hope.

Mr. Guffington (Guffy) and Mr. Belvedere

Chapter 8: Combatting Misery

A Lesson in Overcoming Misery

"Happy people find a way to live with their problems, and miserable people let their problems stop them from living."
Sonya Parker

There is a general rule among most people: "Keep your problems to yourself." Other people have enough problems of their own and don't really have time for yours. It is understood that everybody has something to deal with in this life and that we should generally respect the other person's need to not be bothered. Of course, there are those among us who take the charitable approach and look beyond our own problems and try to help our fellow man. Once we do this, we, sometimes, wished we hadn't. Other people's problems are far worse than ours. Now, if we occupy the profession of a social worker, pastor, or therapist, we are obligated to listen to the other person, and can hopefully offer some sage advice and reasonable solutions to help solve some of their problems. Sometimes, the problems seem endless, and the soul listening feels the complete weight of what the person is going through. They are, however, trained to deal with these situations practically and effectively.

There is one state of being that does not seem to regard these rules or the solutions to these problems. It is known as misery. Misery is defined as a state of great unhappiness or distress. Hard to believe, but there are some people who actually dwell in this state on an ongoing basis! They almost seem to burgeon in misery, even though one never really thrives in unhappiness. No one really wants to be unhappy. It is a choice we make, and we have the power to do something about it. Yet, some *choose* (keyword) misery and carry it around like a shopping bag. Many a discerning person can recognize when someone who possesses this downward, negative state of being comes around them. They either tell them right out not to bring it around, or they choose to avoid this person. I tend to be the former. Bringing that misery around me is like carrying your own rain cloud. I will let you have your moment of unhappiness, but not on a consistent basis because life is too short.

We are living creatures and should be about the business of living. There are so many wonderful experiences and joys in life that we cannot allow setbacks to drive us to a miserable state of being. The sad part about misery is that it seeks out company. This qualifies the practical theory that no one really wants to be miserable and alone. Though no one wants to be alone, we cannot carry this weight into social circles and expect people to rouse and cheer us on. Misery is a state of desolation and despair. So when misery seeks company, it seeks to bring someone else into that state. The individual in a state of misery often does this not realizing how much this can drag someone down. They are sad, so why shouldn't you be sad with them? Misery forgets that people make choices over their lives, yet misery does not care. It is almost determined to bring you down into the pits of isolation, and leave you there. You must not allow this to take place. Misery is a fighter and, in my humble opinion, a weak opponent. It can be struck down by a single action and pushed to the side. When it rears itself again, a good backhanded slap will put it back in its place.

As a verb, combat is when you take action to reduce, prevent, or destroy something undesirable. Misery is the enemy you are combatting, and you, as the other warrior in this battle, must take action! As I stated before, we make choices over our lives, and in this case, it is no different. Misery really puts up a good fight, and if you are not prepared to engage in the battle, you will lose. The interesting aspect of misery that I like (which seems ironic) is that it always makes its presence known. You know when a person, situation, or experience is miserable. Because of this defining feature, you can identify it and gain the upper hand. Misery can be that guest who never leaves. They know they have worn out their welcome, but they continue to linger. Know this, if you are to combat misery, you must engage in some form of action! An unusual way that I learned about how to deal with what could be considered miserable situations was through a cat that drifted into my life for a short season.

His name was Bellows. It was the fall of 1997. By a standard definition, Bellows would be considered a stray cat. Feral cats are cats that are born to other feral cats or stray cats. There is usually little or no human interaction. Their contact with humans comes in the form of them congregating around a person's home or some other dwelling where there may be food and some degree of shelter. I knew Bellows was different and had lived with humans at some point in his life. He possessed a certain domestic training that those other cats did not have. Bellows was a beautiful gray-white calico that, when I look back in hindsight, was a stray. He did have a penchant for hanging with the neighborhood feral cats. I made the all too often mistake of giving him some food and water, and the next thing I knew, I had a constant visitor. I did not mind because he was no trouble and he was actually very friendly. Of course, I was not about to take on his feral cronies and start a soup kitchen for feral cats in the community. The feral cats that hung around our neighborhood were a troublesome bunch. Making noises all hours of the night, especially when they wanted to reproduce. They would rifle through trash and make themselves comfortable in small spaces under people's homes or in their garages. Most times, they would sleep all day and wander the streets at night. I used to see them all the time when I went to work or when I was just working around the house. I am sure the neighbors called animal control, but they had even outsmarted the city. They knew how to plot and plan and mastered avoiding being caught.

It did break my heart to see these animals out there like that, especially when they produced a litter or two. Then it was gut-wrenching because now there were innocent, defenseless kittens. Bellows did not seem to relegate himself to this type of behavior. I often wondered if there was some feral female he was interested in. There was not. Because of the design of our houses, I would often hear my neighbors screaming or throwing something at these cats to get them to leave. Bellows saw and heard all of this commotion, and he seemed to make himself quite comfortable on my doorstep. I kept giving him fresh water and dry food, and he always had a good appetite. I would often observe those cats and would think to myself, "What a miserable life they are living." They have no place to call home. They don't know where their next meal is coming from that day. And when the elements were bad, they really had to employ defense tactics to protect themselves. Though I had a heart for their plight, I knew, at that time, I could not save all these pitiful creatures. Watching Bellows, though, was an interesting lesson to be learned from the animal world and one that I could certainly utilize in dealing with human beings who seemed to wallow in misery. Remember what I said about taking action. Bellows did just that.

As the months went by, the other feral cats would watch Bellows and seem to say to themselves, "He has got it good over there with that guy, getting food and water any time he wants. What makes him so special?" They wanted to encroach their misery on poor Bellows as he lay in my backyard or on my front porch. He would also come in at certain times and stay over if it was raining or cold outside. I welcomed my furry friend, and he knew I cared. One particular morning, these cats were wailing, known as caterwauling, something terrible outside my window. They woke me up. I went to look outside my window and saw an interesting sight. There was a gang of cats surrounding Bellows as if they were going to take him out and take over his free meal plan. Bellows (in what was very distinctive in his personality) was like "I'm not having it. Step over here if you want to, but it won't be pretty." The leader of that gang of cats rolled the dice and tried to hiss his bluff. Bellows took his stand at my back doorstep and, in a move that I have only seen in the WWE, grabbed that cat by the back of his neck and body slammed him several times. The other cats backed up really quick. I ran outside immediately to break up this animal violence. The other cats fled, and their poor leader of the pack ran away like a scaredy-cat. Bellows looked up at me as if to say, "I'm good. Now may I have some water?"

Though this may seem like an over-the-top lesson in combatting misery, you must understand what I was observing in this moment. This fight may be a common practice among feral cats. Bellows had found something good with me. Even if it was for a short while, his life was good. He was happy. Those other cats were sad and miserable. They were trying to bring that misery to his situation and make it worse. I was not going to be able to care for eight to ten feral cats hanging around my house. It was not fair to me. I could only do the responsible thing in trying to get them to a local animal shelter, but they did not want that, and I did not want that for them. I wished for them to live in forever homes with someone who could take on providing a safe, loving environment for those cats. The point here is that Bellows took action in not letting misery come in and mess up his environment. He had found a small piece of happiness and wanted to preserve and enjoy it. Bellows left shortly thereafter, and I never saw him again.

Reflective Thought

There is a saying: "Into every life, some rain must fall." Well, one of those rainstorms comes in the form of misery. The only thing about this type of rainstorm is that you can see it when it is coming or before it comes. The key is what you will do with your proverbial umbrella when the rain hits. No one likes to get caught in a rainstorm. You like to have some type of protection or shelter against it. In knowing this, you prepare yourself for the coming storm. Unlike the meteorologist, where they can make accurate predictions about the weather, you cannot predict when misery is coming. You will know, however, when it is present. There is an effective way to handle misery. Some people may receive help through support and counseling. Others may just need a shoulder to cry on in those moments of misery. When the cry is over, they can feel better about the situation or experience. Then, there are those among us who simply have no time for misery and its lack of merit. We shut it down right at the point of impact. This all depends on the individual. You can combat misery – and win! You can put it in its place and move on with your life. We all will have moments of sadness and despair. We choose to look up, dust ourselves off, and continue on in the journey of life.

Chapter 9: A Mother's Love

A Lesson on a Mother's Love

"A mother's love is a reflection of God's love."
Isaiah 66:13

The North American bison is a fascinating creature. Known historically as "buffalo," these mammoth creatures are distant relatives to the buffalo. Bison are the largest terrestrial animals in America and have some major distinctions that define their species. They are excellent swimmers and can cross rivers over 800 meters long. They are very nomadic and travel in herds. The male bison, known as bulls, usually leave their female counterparts to join an all-male herd. The female herds tend to be smaller, but no less tight knit. The females are also very protective of their young, the calves.

One of the main predators of the bison is the gray wolf. Though their size, compared to the bison is much smaller, they are no less intimidated by this massive creature. Their strategy is to chase after the herds and use the technique of "divide and conquer." It is their objective to separate one bison from the herd. If it is a female and she is still nursing her young, her overprotective nature will not let her separate from her calf, let alone leave him at the mercy of these carnivorous beasts. The wolves are crafty. They possess a certain patience in stalking their prey and know just when to pounce to separate a lone bison. A mother bison, who, in size alone, could easily ravage her predator, must stand when she is separated to fight two, maybe three wolves at one time. Her instincts are to survive. She also knows that her young calf will be helpless against such predators.

As the pursuit ensues, the herd run with unwavering speed to the higher plains. As a group, they can take their predators on, yet they seek to get away to higher plains to dismiss an ongoing battle. The wolves run alongside the herd, taunting and biting at them to try to bring them down. It would almost seem they have succeeded when two of the herd are separated. The mother will not go down without a fight. She constantly doubles-back in the protection of her young. At some point, the young calf must learn to fight, but this skill is taught over time, not when they are outnumbered and under attack. The mother bison can easily maim the gray wolf with a kick of her hoof. Also, their heads can be described as "massive battering rams." This mother will not let her calf alone. She will fiercely protect and fight for him. The young calf is careful to stay by his mother and, in extreme measures, learns to use his own hoof to fight off his predator.

Such devotion in this species is translated into many others as it pertains to the female bison and her young. Many mothers would sacrifice their lives if it meant their offspring would live. The herd is still nearby, and when the predators are warded off, she listens for their stampede in an effort to rejoin them. She knew that, no matter what these predators' intentions, she was not going to go down without a fight. It will take everything in her to fight off these vicious foes, and whether she is tired, or even hungry, the safety and well-being of her offspring takes priority. Now that is a mother's love. In the end, mother and calf are reunited with their herd and feel the safety of a group from which they did not want to be separated.

What is it about a mother's love that makes for such an incredible bond between her and her child? This has been the subject of many studies and fascinated researchers for years. Studies done at McGill University have shown that, in testing rats, when they nursed their pups during infancy, they tended to develop and become less nervous than the ones they didn't. This goes to show how nurturing during those formative years helps develop future characteristics. No mother wants to see her child in trouble. She wants to prepare them for whatever may befall them in their lives, even if it's within the ranks of their own species. Male gorillas tend to be very stand-offish from their young, especially the males. The mother, though embraced by her male companion, must pay special attention to her young. The male's dominance in the band is so strong that they tend to want to hurt, or even kill, the young gorilla. This is when the mother goes into protection overdrive. She will fight the male leader when it comes to protecting her young. It would almost seem unimaginable that the male gorilla, who is the father, would want to hurt his own. These interesting analogies give us an interesting perspective into human mothers.

I know many women who are mothers. For them, the sheer joy of childbirth and the nurture and care of their young is their main priority. Whether they are single, married, in a domestic partnership, or some other unconventional family structure, they form an immediate bond with their newborn. There almost seems to be an unspoken contract formed between the two that says, "No matter what you do, where you go, what you grow to become, I will always be here for you. I am your mother." That is an amazing contract that the child always carries throughout his life because, although it was unspoken in the beginning of his/her life, when they are older, it speaks volumes. No matter what life brings you, a young man knows he can always go to his mother. Fathers do form strong bonds with their daughters because they tend to be the first male figure in their lives. Even a daughter recognizes her mother's wit, strength, and devotion. These characteristics become more evident to her when she herself becomes a mother.

It is a fascinating observation to watch any species within the animal kingdom when they reproduce. It teaches us about the evolution of life, yet we see so much of ourselves, as humans, in these beautiful acts of nature. When a human mother sees that bond between another species and her offspring, there is an immediate relatability factor. The silent nod that says, "Yes, mama, I know what is happening between you and your offspring. I, too, have had this experience with my own. I understand you completely." That is a pretty amazing trait between both animals and humans alike.

Reflective Thought

In this life, we are only given one mother. Yes, we may have surrogate mothers and godmothers, but no one can ever replace the woman who gave you life. From the moment you were born, your mother's instinct was to love and protect you. She watched you as you grew and developed. She ran to your side when you fell on the playground to tend to your scraped knee. She protected you from the bullies that threatened your life as a young adult, and she stood by you when life's hardest moments seemed to weigh you down. Her love, like God's love, is undying and unconditional. It is that love that carries you through your darkest hours and sweetest moments. These same traits are echoed within the animal kingdom from a mother to her offspring. A simple observation of the species proves this fact to be true. Mothers are unique creations that God carefully weaved into the fabric of human (and animal) kind. Treasure her, the one who gave YOU life, as she goes through this life. There may be times when you feel, as a grown up, you don't need your mother. Nothing could be further from the truth. We will always need our mothers. And if she is taken away from us at a certain age, know this. She has placed within you everything you will ever need to carry you through your life. This gift may be further developed by other important figures in your life, but your mother is the one who placed it within you first. It was almost as if there was a fair exchange from the hand of God to the heart of a mother and then onto you. She is irreplaceable, and there will never be another like her.

Chapter 10: A Moment of Joy

A Lesson in Joy

"If you carry joy in your heart, you can heal any moment."
Carlos Santana

I believe we have all experienced a moment of joy. Joy, that feeling of great pleasure and happiness, can be ignited by a number of different things. The birth of a child. The purchase of a new home. The completion of an educational experience. These moments can incite happiness in a person. They can carry this happiness for weeks, even years at a time. This happiness is not defined by external circumstances, but comes from within the individual and gives us pause to really examine what causes a person to be happy. When I used to work at Universal Studios in Hollywood, I had a particular co-worker who always intrigued me. We were all trained to exceed guests' expectations and go beyond the call of duty, if need be. This co-worker of mine did that, and so much more. That wasn't what intrigued me though. It was the fact that he always had a smile on his face. I can barely recall a moment when I did not see him smile. I used to ask myself, "Why does he always seems to wear a permanent smile?" I later found out that it was his job. He genuinely loved his job. It made him very happy to be at work and do whatever he could for the guests at the park. We all thought we were doing the same until some of us retreated to the break room and we saw and heard how people were really feeling. This was not to disparage how people felt, for they were just being honest, just as my co-worker had an honest love for his job. I respected him for that. He always seemed to carry this joyful spirit wherever he went. It is one thing to experience a moment of joy. It is a totally different story when you carry that joy all the time.

I have been captivated with another particular mammal that lives among us. Dolphins have intrigued me since my childhood from the days of watching *Flipper* to my experiences with them in sea life. I have never been a proponent of any animal being encased for show. There is something about an animal being free and able to live that freedom in their own natural habitat. Dolphins, for some reason, have adapted to these particular situations and have not allowed it to dampen their spirits or their personalities. Dolphins are a member of the order of Cetacean, which places them in the group of other diverse aquatic mammals, such as porpoises and whales. Dolphins, in a social order, like to travel in groups known as pods. These pods can be as little as twelve dolphins to what is also referred to as "super pods," where the number of dolphins can exceed one thousand. Dolphins are extremely social animals, and they can form strong social bonds with one another. They have been known to stay with an injured or ill dolphin, even bringing them to the surface to breathe. As a helper to humans, they can also ward off predators in the sea (i.e. sharks) by swimming circles around a swimmer to keep the sharks away. Through the use of sonar, avid seaman and Coast Guard patrols are usually aware when there are pods of dolphins nearby. What is most fascinating about them is that they appear to be helpers of the sea. There is a connection of this mammal to other mammals in the sea and on land that strikes the heart of our curiosity to learn more about them. They communicate with clicks through echolocation to have a sense of their surroundings. In communicating with their own species, they "whistle." It is thought that each dolphin has his own "signature whistle" to identify one another. Marine biologists have studied and continue to study dolphins for behavior patterns and research into their physiological makeup. The studies help them understand the species better and how this research can be translated into human patterns of life.

If you have ever looked at a dolphin up close, it seems like they have a permanent smile on their faces. Though they have other ways of communicating, this smile seems to radiate from them with such exuberance and delight. I have seen dolphins up close, and they seem happiest when they are in their social groups with one another. Their interaction with humans is undeniably real and heartfelt. They come to trust humans and form the kindest friendship with them, especially their individual trainers. It is here that you see that wide smile on their faces that signifies they are happy. Their response level is even heightened to the point that, if they could, they would jump out of the water and shake your hand with their fins.

So how does one measure a moment of joy, if joy is that feeling of great pleasure or happiness and our lives are measured in moments? It would seem that we would have to carry this joy with us all the time. Moments occur all the time in our lives, and those moments cannot be limited by the absence of one feeling or another. So we carry this joy with us all the time. The opening quote by Carlos Santana, which states, "If we carry joy in our heart, we can heal any moment," is very true. There will be external circumstances that may dictate how you act or react in a particular moment, but if you carry joy with you, it is like an eternal flame that never goes out. No one can ever take away the joy that you feel in your heart. And when those moments require something as simple as a smile, your heart can be immersed in that joy. I believe that only God can give us that kind of joy. You carry this kind of joy in your heart, and it can give you strength when you need it and carry you through some of life's toughest moments. How wonderful to possess that?

When we look at our dolphin friends, we can see there is something about them that seems joyous and exuberant. They seem to bask in the coolness of the water as they look for opportunities where they can help someone or even another creature of the sea. Dolphins carry their joy, and no matter where you see them, it is always expressed on their faces. Having had a chance to be up close and personal with a dolphin allowed me to see this joy radiate from them. And if you had the opportunity to toss them a piece of fish, they would do a flip in a heartbeat that showed you gratitude and endless happiness. The part I love about dolphins is that, when you have moments like this, they seem to want to share that joy with you. They want to invite you into their space, and it appears as if they are saying, "It does not matter what is going on in your life because you can be happy." I think that is why we get that feeling of excitement when they do that back flip or incredible "tail walk" on the water. You cannot help but take in that moment and smile.

Reflective Thought

Someone calls you and tells you that you just won a major sweepstakes. After you prove that the call is valid and you have indeed won, you are swept up in a floodgate of emotions. One of those emotions is joy. You may cry, run, or even start screaming to express this joy. No matter how excited you may get, that feeling will not last always. Why? It was a momentary feeling created by an external circumstance in something you know will not bring you complete happiness. Watch how fast that feeling fades when you realize Uncle Sam is waiting in the wings to take his part. Or when unexpected expenses seem to magically appear, just when you thought you had it made. All temporal. Yet, in this life, you can have an abundance of joy that can be carried in your heart to make every moment a lasting one. Animals (dolphins, in particular) seem to possess it. As they swim through the water with purpose and determination, they are also happy about who they are and seem to be intent on bringing that happiness to whomever they make contact. When that contact is made, you will feel the joy they have as it ignites something in you. You also feel this when you are with your family and friends. You feel this when you are on a well-deserved vacation. You carry this joy always, and the true moment of joy comes when you know it was given by God, and any other moment in your life can be a joyous one.

Chapter 11: From the Ruins There Came a Shadough

A Lesson in Compassion/Gentleness

By Deidre McBride Johnson

"Constant kindness can accomplish much. As the sun makes ice melt, kindness causes misunderstanding, mistrust and hostility to evaporate."
Albert Schweitzer

It is hard to imagine anyone or anything being abused. It forms a terrible image in the mind, often one we cannot escape. To actually watch an abusive situation stirs up so much within the observer. There are hints of anger, frustration, and hatred. You are angry because you see this type of behavior being inflicted upon another person, and you know it's wrong. You are frustrated because, depending on the situation, there may not be much you can do. It incites hatred because abuse devalues the abused, and you feel an intense dislike for the abuser. Let me point out that the abused person's life is still worth so much more. Due to this horrific situation, the abused person feels worthless. Often, the abuse takes place behind closed doors, and many of us are not privy to its horrific effects until it is too late. Then, there are the extremely high number of cases that are not even reported. Statistics have shown that over fifty percent of cases are never reported. This makes it harder to know exactly how much abuse is going on.

Abuse develops fear, fear that often cannot be escaped. It is a fear that stays with an individual or creature for a lifetime. It is only in the presence of love that this fear can be quelled. The sad part about abused persons is that they carry it, and to the untrained eye, it would seem like everything is all right. One would have to pay very close attention to a person or living creature to detect signs of abuse. Someone who has been delivered from an abusive situation can recognize the signs of a person currently involved in an abusive relationship. Upon recognition, an individual may be prompted to say or do something to, hopefully, help. This may not always be the case. The big difference between the abuse of a human and the abuse of an animal is that an animal does not have a voice to cry out for help. Oftentimes, this poor creature withdraws himself in cowering fear that no one would recognize unless they have seen the animal in a distressful situation. It is heartbreaking to know that there are hundreds of these precious creatures facing this horrific treatment with almost no sign of help or hope.

The emotional pain that follows abuse is horrendous. Physical pain that is inflicted, though it is wrong, can be healed. Emotional pain goes so much deeper. There is a depth to it that would almost seem insurmountable to get over. Emotional pain brings on depression, anxiety, conflict, and, sometimes, the worst of all, death. What would cause another person to do this to a fellow human being or, in another case scenario, a precious animal? The person causing this is also in a great state of pain himself. This form of projection makes it worse for the abused and the abuser. The picture that is painted almost seems destroyed. When we see such depredation where it would almost seem impossible to find anything good coming out of it, we learn of a story that has to be told where hope still lives. Such was the case with Shadough, a beautiful Shitzu that was facing this awful state of being.

Deidre is an independent woman who had been on her own since her early twenties. She has always appreciated having her own space. Though not a selfish individual, she has always been open to sharing her space with another living creature. She had already parted with her beloved cocker spaniel because the building she moved to would not allow pets. The thought of another separation with one more pet was too much for her heart to bear at this time. She had given herself time and space after the separation of her other dog and had moved on with her life. Her job was quite demanding. She had already raised her son, and her independence was a welcome refresher to her life. She worked in a multi-complex facility where the essence of her work involved property management. She would often receive calls about a particular unit on the property that would involve her office. She was not expecting the call that was about to come to her office this day and change to her life.

They brought in a stray dog that was cold and shivering. He cowered in fear as the other workers reached out to help him. Their presence made him shy away even more. Deidre, having had a dog before, knew how to properly approach this poor creature without increasing his fear. She spoke to him in a calm, soothing tone and made eye contact with him. She noticed the sadness in his eyes. Someone had done wrong by him, and Deidre knew it. She also noticed that he responded to her voice and soon became relaxed. It was here that Deidre saw a faint smile on the dog's face, and she knew, in that instant, that he was the one who was to change her state of independence back to being a pet parent again. She took him home with her (which was a violation of her lease), and the next day, she took him to the vet. He received the proper medical treatment. He was thoroughly examined and found to be healthy. The doctor, however, knew that he had been abused, hence his fearful state of being. He was also not microchipped, which would make it very hard to track down his owner. Deidre was glad for that because she did not want to give him up and had already set her heart on keeping him.

The building in which Deidre lived clearly had a "no pet policy." Deidre knew that anything worth having was worth fighting for in this life. She is a strong woman who will stand for what she believes in, and who has come up against the best of them. She knew she had rights living within her building and was not about to see this precious creature hauled off to the shelter. She explained to the management the situation with the dog, whom she had appropriately named Shadough. She felt he was a unique dog who deserved a unique name. She became his voice from what was obviously a traumatic and emotionally painful situation for him. She knew, if he was turned over to the shelter, and no one claimed him, his days there would be numbered. Deidre was not about to let that happen. After clearly outlining her reasons for keeping him, the management had a change of heart for Shadough. It was decided that, because of the way he had been abandoned and abused, he should not have to go through that experience again. He was not going to. He was added to Deidre's lease and began his new life in his forever home with the woman who saw in those sad eyes a dog who deserved better and a new life. She was able to open that space of solitude and give Shadough the life that was needed for him.

For the first few days, he did not eat or drink any water, so there was deep concern that Shadough might become ill or dehydrated. Deidre became very sensitive to this sweet pup and came down on the floor with him. She allowed him to eat the food straight from her hands. When he was done, he would graciously lick her hand. It was a very special bonding moment for these two, as Shadough had come out of a dark place, a place of fear and neglect. He did not deserve that. And to be left alone in a cold, empty apartment, not knowing who or what may come for him probably terrified the poor creature. He found hope in Deidre's eyes and in her voice. It was a comfort to him that was like a soothing balm. Shadough's heart had a found a home, and Deidre was more than willing to open hers to him.

Reflective Thought

So often we hear the reports of abused children, elders, spouses, and animals. Abuse in any form is wrong and should not have to be endured by anyone. We live in a world where people can be free from such horrific behavior. Acts of abuse go so far beyond the present situation, and it affects more than just the abused. A child who sees his mother being abused carries this with him for life. A neglected senior, who should be living their golden years in peace and satisfaction, may feel helpless and alone. So it is with animals. Dogs, cats, livestock, and even fowl should never be subjected to any form of abuse. They deserve to live a life of dignity and care, just as humans do. As in any case of abuse, animals carry these deep wounds for a lifetime. They should not have to do that. Their healing comes from people who extend their hand and heart to rescue and help them by bringing them out of these awful situations and into a life of hope and love. These precious creatures do not have a voice when they are rescued. If you listen with your heart, you will hear their voices of thanks and gratitude.

(Reflection written by Hartford Hough)

Chapter 12: Through Thick and Thin

A Lesson in Faithfulness

"I'm on your side
When times are hard
And you need some understanding

I'm on your side
When times gets rough
And no one else can care enough
I'm on your side to be for you"
from the song "I'm On Your Side" by Narada Michael Walden

I find it very interesting that, for some people, when life gets hard, they want to quit, just go by the side of the road and get out of the race. I learned something very true from some of my married friends. They informed me that, once the marriage ceremony is over, the real work begins. I was pretty certain of this because I know the honeymoon can't last forever. The thing about most people is that they take too much for granted, and when "real work" is in front of them, they want to quit. They become lazy. They assume things are just going to work themselves out in the end, failing to realize that they must put some effort into the task before them. Marriage, like our places of employment, is a day-to-day job. You must work at it and be faithful to it. In doing so, you will also reap the many benefits from it: a loving partner, beautiful children, a well-maintained household, and so much more. Standing by your partner is the essence of being faithful. It shows love and true devotion.

One of the saddest stories in the Bible, in my opinion, is the story of Job. His story, in itself, was not so sad, as much as it was tragic. Job was blessed and prospered under the mighty hand of God. He knew from whence his blessings came, and he was always ready to offer thanks unto God for His provision. When the enemy sought to destroy Job's faith in God, God told him, "He is in thy hand, take everything but his life." The sad part for me was Job's wife. When tragedy befell him, the man had lost everything. You would think that the person to whom he was betrothed would stand by his side until the end. Instead, this woman uttered the words, "You are still going to maintain your integrity before Him? Curse God and die!" Ouch! What would cause someone to speak such words, especially when you are down on everything. Could it be that she was more connected to the "things" that Job had than she was to her husband? Her faithfulness failed that day. She left her husband in his worst possible state.

Being faithful means "continual service," being unwavering in your affection to the person, cause, or group you are standing with. It is this kind of faithfulness that speaks untold volumes in a relationship. For, you see, no matter how much you think you are not being observed, you really are. People are impressed when they see relationships "that work" and "that are working." It is an inspiration to many that gives them hope for their own chance at finding someone or becoming involved in a cause that makes a difference. When people see this, it makes the heart glad. For example, when you hear of a couple that have been together for over fifty years, what an amazing testament to marriage. Realizing that, in that marriage, though, there were certainly ups and downs, they made it through, and they are still standing as a testament to weathering the storms they encountered. Such faithfulness also comes when animals are tested in their loyalty to their owners.

The video was heart-wrenching. No names were given, but the simplicity of this video and the actors involved played it so well, you knew exactly what they were saying and the message came through very clear. The old man heard his alarm clock. He was awakened by its sound. His furry companion jumped on his bed to encourage him to get up. He did not fight him, for he knew it was time to rise and get ready for their day. In different scenes in the video, we see the old man making breakfast, meeting his friends for coffee, running his errands with a stop at the local market. All the while, his furry companion is right there by his side. You can tell in this video, the dog has the heart of the old man, and the old man has the heart of his dog. He truly loves him for being in his life.

One night, the man becomes ill and suffers a heart attack. The paramedics arrive, and they place the old man in the ambulance. His furry companion attempts to climb on board, but they close the door on him. This does not deter him, for he runs after the ambulance all the way to the hospital. He attempts to go in after they arrive, but the door is again closed in his face. What follows are scenes of many days where the dog is standing vigil outside the hospital. All day. All night. He never leaves. Even when it begins to rain, he finds shelter under a bushel and continues to watch the door of that hospital, faithfully waiting for the old man to come out. People in the hospital see the dog, but no one bothers him as he stands vigil. He probably eats from scraps of food he can find to keep his strength, but all the while, he maintains a faithful eye on that hospital door.

In the last scene of the video, something extraordinary happens. The hospital door opens, and a young lady is wheeled outside after having had surgery. The dog does not know her, but he recognizes something else in her. She has received a heart transplant. We draw the conclusion that the old man has passed, and this woman was in line to receive a new heart from a donor (the old man). His dog immediately runs up and jumps on the young lady, showing her love and affection because he knows the heart he was always faithful to now abides in this young lady. She does not shoo him away, but it is apparent she welcomes him to become her new companion.

What I loved about this video and the story was that this dog was faithful and remained in "continual service" to his owner. No matter what happened in the course of a day, he was willing to do the work of a faithful companion. He never wavered in that, and this made for an amazing story of standing by the old man's side, even as he was dying. Yet, the beauty of his organ being donated was that the dog knew it now was beating in another life, and he would continue to follow it always.

Reflective Thought

If you have ever been blessed to have a best friend, you know the boundless energy that draws you two together. You also know that, no matter what happens, this person will always have your back. If you have had a friend since childhood and you grew up through the years, this becomes a testament to the timeless quality of a friendship. You went to school together, graduated, participated in each other's weddings, were there for the birth of each other's children (probably became the godparents), went through the hills and valleys of life. Both of you have seen good times and bad. You saw the victories and counted the losses. No matter what, you were always there for each other. Friendships that truly last a lifetime are gifts from God. People can be so fickle in their relationships. They can be dubbed "fair-weather friends." They go whichever way the wind blows, and you find their loyalty is not always with you. That is okay. People are going to be people. There is no written law that says everyone you meet will be your best friend. However, if you do have that one person (and they may be your husband or wife), TREASURE THEM! Never let a day go by without saying you love them. Never let the sun go down on your wrath. Never take them for granted. The aforementioned video was an example of an older, single man and his dog that illustrated this point vividly. And be it animal or human, always appreciate them. That is the joy of having someone go with you "through the thick and the thin."

Chapter 13: A Thing of Beauty

A Lesson in Appreciating All Things Beautiful

"A thing of beauty is a joy forever."
"Endymion"
John Keats

How beautiful are the things that surround us? We should see (notice I said "should") beautiful things, objects, nature, and, yes, people all the time. They surround us, yet we so often walk by them, ignoring their allure. Sometimes, there has to almost be that "pie slap in the face" moment for us to take notice of something beautiful. Other times, it may take another individual to point it out to us. Either way, the beauty that surrounds us has a significant meaning. *People* magazine does an issue every year where they name the Most Beautiful People. It may not necessarily be physical beauty (although it usually is a deciding factor), but they also make their decisions based on personality, style, humanitarianism, and generosity. They often put over one hundred people on this list. I have so often seen this issue of the magazine, and though I do not know the people they name personally, based on their contributions to society through film, television, sports, politics, and the arts, their list is subjectively accurate. Only people who really know those on the list can make that honest, fair statement about the person. In the court of public opinion, we may see a particular personality who was caught in an awful vice or some other form of bad behavior. We wonder, "What in the world are they doing on this list?" Yet, they are. And though they may have done something wrong, it can hardly diminish them and say they are less beautiful. All creatures are beautiful. I came to appreciate this beauty at a very young age, and I still carry that admiration in my heart for the beauty of all things.

Many years ago, my aunt would do something very special for my grandmother (her mother) and me. My aunt Rose was a strong, independent woman who prided herself on being able to stand on her own two feet. Even after coming through a messy divorce and having to go out and work for herself, she always came out on top. She also had a very generous heart, which was a trait I know she acquired from my grandmother. She loved her mother and her only nephew (at that particular time). She was always looking for ways to give back to her and make her feel special as my grandmother was getting on in years. To me, this was a beautiful way to honor the woman who gave her life. I saw this act carried out so many times in my life, and it always made me smile.

On a glorious Saturday morning, my aunt invited me and Grandma to go on a trip with her. She was going to take us on an outing to a place they were both familiar with but was a new location I had never been. I was nine years old at the time, and I loved spending time with my grandmother. My aunt always had special places of interest to take us that she and my grandmother could always appreciate, and I would treasure the memories in my heart. She would come to pick us up early because she wanted to get a head start on the road and avoid traffic. I can recall that Saturday morning when she drove up to our house with that tan Ford Grenada. I liked her car. I have to admit, though I loved my aunt, she was the slowest driver this side of creation. As we drove off from the house, it seemed like endless hours before we reached the interstate. Nonetheless, I was glad to be on the outing. Grandma had made some sandwiches and fried chicken. She always packed a hearty lunch and made sure we were full when it came time for consumption. I loved that about her. I sat in the backseat while they chatted away in the front about life, family, church, and friends. I knew about half of what they were talking about, and the rest of the time, I enjoyed watching the scenery from the car as we drove up the interstate. Every now and then, my aunt would ask me a question about something, and I would give her the best answer a nine-year-old could give. As I recall that time of questions, I now see that she was preparing me mentally for what I was about to experience for the first time.

We arrived at the Sterling Gardens in Tuxedo, New York, a little late. It was still bright and sunny and considerably warm for October, but it did not matter because the place was teeming with people, and it looked like it was going to be a nice, enjoyable day. After she parked the car, we got out and headed toward the entrance to the gardens. I noticed, though there were a handful of other children, it was mostly adults. I said to myself, "Okay. This is not Disneyland." I took my grandmother's hand, and she led me into the park. My grandmother was still in good health and agile for her age, so she still walked very quickly when moving about. I had to keep up. As we entered the park, I was struck by a bevy of floral arrangements. I saw flowers, flowers, and more flowers. Now this may not have been the most appealing thing for a nine-year-old, but there was something quite fascinating about all these floral arrangements. They were indeed beautiful to look at. My aunt, who was always carrying her trusty Kodak camera, stopped us several times to capture a photo in front of a lovely spray of flowers. My grandmother, who was very knowledgeable about nurseries and plants, would stop me often and explain what a particular flower was. I have to admit, I wasn't completely bored at this time, but then something very special happened.

As we continued to walk around the gardens, I noticed a crowd of people gathering in this one spot. I figured there was some type of attraction, and I prodded my aunt and grandmother to walk in the direction of the gathering crowd. As we assembled in this one area, there was a small fence, and it was surrounded by the most beautiful arrangement of floral magnificence. What I was about to see was to be even more spectacular than those flowers. I noticed a very large bird walking around in the fenced area. I also noticed that everyone was getting their cameras ready to take a picture. In my mind, I kept saying, "It's just a bird, and he is not doing anything." My aunt came over and explained to me that the bird we were looking at was named a peacock, and if we remained very still, something beautiful was about to happen. The bird stood about three feet tall with a blue body and a slender neckline. We waited there for about ten minutes, and then it happened. This bird opened its tail into a beautiful fan of artistic genius. I saw red and blue feathers lined up so evenly in this marvelous spread of glory. There were specks of gold and black within its tail. The peacock walked around for several minutes as cameras shuttered away. The people were mesmerized by this creature's magnificent beauty, and so was I. I loved looking at this bird. This wonderful creature of beauty had me spellbound. I watched as he strutted with pride, knowing he was being watched and adored. I fell in love with the peacock that day. Ever since then, whenever I see one, I hold on with deep hope that he will open that glorious tail once again.

The sight of this beautiful animal and God's artistic flair in making him made me see the beauty that always surrounds us.

Reflective Thought

The one thing that people do so often is take something for granted. We just assume someone or something will always be there. When it is taken away, we become angry or sad because we realize that it will not be coming back. This is why we must not take for granted the beauty that surrounds us. We can, if we look carefully, see it every day and appreciate its splendor. When God took the time to create certain animals, He knew what an impressive sight they would be, as well as a reflection of His glory. If you have never seen the tail of a peacock open in all its array, you are missing something spectacular. Or witnessed a herd of horses running across a field in timeless unity. Or a school of fish in the ocean swimming as if they were drawing a painting. If you ever have the privilege to see it, you will know you are catching another glimpse of the handiwork of the Creator and how wonderful it is to be in its presence. When He created the fowls of the air and those on land, each one was tapped with the finger of His love that makes them unique and very beautiful. He saw that "it was good." When God created man, He made him a marvelous creation and saw that "it was very good."

Chapter 14: The Power of Knowing

A Lesson in Awareness

"Knowledge is Power."

Sir Francis Bacon

Many of us who grew up in the sixties remember the popular sitcom *Bewitched*. The perennial television show featured the fictitious character Mrs. Kravitz. She was the noisy neighbor who seemed to be in everyone's business but her own. She was especially infatuated with what happened in the Stevens household and could not wait to report it to anyone who would listen to her gossip about a current situation with them. Now there are some who would consider Mrs. Kravitz's gossip a bad thing because it seemed like she was doing too much meddling. On the surface, that is what it may have appeared to be. There is no real merit in gossip. However, there was an interesting aspect about Mrs. Kravitz's behavior that could be viewed differently. Though she always got caught in these odd predicaments with Samantha and Darren, she wasn't making things up. She had knowledge of what was really going on. Sometimes bringing out the truth about a matter is often hindered by many conflicts. She was only trying to make others aware of what she had seen or heard, and of course, this resulted in funny hijinks that made for a delightful comedy.

There is something about having information that really does empower an individual. Most people are not looking to be on a power trip, but harnessing themselves with any information does just that. It empowers you to be knowledgeable and helps you plan your next course of action. We look at the news, and information is disseminated about current events, sports, and weather. This information governs how we actually behave. If the meteorologist says there will be rain tomorrow, we carry an umbrella. If we are informed that our favorite sports team has not been doing so well, we probably won't make preparations for the playoffs. We laughed at Mrs. Kravitz because she was only trying to tell the information that she had become aware of, and sitcoms have an over–the-top way of bringing this out.

I can recall taking a trip on a cruise a few years ago. I still marveled at the navigational skills of the captain. He was made aware of a storm that was directly in our path. He knew we could not go through the storm because there would be rough waters, and we would be completely thrown off course. He was already dealing with several passengers who had become ill, due to seasickness. What he did was carefully chart out the map that set us on a slightly different course. He informed us as what was happening (Of course, half the people were probably on the main deck playing a sport or eating something). He navigated the ship so well that many of us did not even notice what was happening. All we saw was the beautiful ocean and sunlit skies that made our trip that much more enjoyable. It was especially pleasing if you were sitting in the upper deck lounge because you saw the beauty and magnificence of the ocean. Had he not been made aware of the pending storm, it could have proven disastrous.

Living in California has taught me quite a lot. I have learned that, when we have wildfires, they affect the domain for wildlife, and they, sometimes, have to come down to suburbia in search of food, especially if they are nursing. I have also learned that, even though emergency personnel informed us that we live in earthquake country, we need to prepare ourselves for the "big one" that could strike at any time. I also learned (and am not surprised) that many people are not prepared in the least. They just assume it will be a small tremor, and they will brave it out with not one flashlight or battery to their names. Yet, when something happens, they all want to rush to the Home Depot and Lowe's to grab the necessary supplies. Instead of just preparing themselves, they would rather chance it. It happened one night when we had a major power outage. Of course, half of my neighbors didn't even have a candle. All they could do was sleep that one out, for there was no power. How do you handle a situation that the meteorologist can't necessarily predict but your animals can?

Seismologists are scientists who study earthquakes and the propagation of elastic waves throughout the earth. They can track and monitor this natural phenomenon through computers and seismographs. They track these waves through graphs and charts. What I find fascinating, though, is that they cannot accurately predict when it will happen. They can only "guesstimate" when a possible tremor will occur. If that is not bad enough, then we have to deal with the "aftershocks." Sometimes these can cause more damage than the initial earthquake. It is something that those of us who live on the West Coast have come to deal with. It is still unnerving when the earth beneath you shakes and you have no control. However, I have come to realize I have one up on the seismologists of the day, and I am sure anyone who has animals can attest to this truth.

It has been said cats possess a "sixth sense" about future events, the spirit realm, and the weather. On July 29, 2008, the Los Angeles area had a 5.5 magnitude earthquake that rocked the city, especially those of us who lived near the epicenter. This particular quake, known as the "2008 Chino Hills earthquake," certainly set the ground in motion for many. I am proud to say that two my cats, Guffy and Charity, knew well in advance something was about to happen. Knowing their behavior patterns as I do, I always pay close attention when they start "acting unusual or strange." For the most part, this is not normal. It is a signal that something could be wrong. The initial quake hit about 2:15 am, and I am glad to say, I slept right through it. However, it was at about 4:08 am when they started acting different. About one minute later, Charity jumped onto my bed and woke me up. It was her hard pounce on my stomach that caused me to get up right away. I noticed that Guffy was moving around the house in an unusual fashion. It was as if he were saying, "You better get up, man. Something is about to happen." So I got up. When the actual aftershock (which registered 3.8 on the Richter scale) happened, I felt it. Thank God there was no considerable damage that I saw. I immediately turned on the television, and wouldn't you know it — a breaking news story was coming on. "The Los Angeles area has just been hit with what appears to be an aftershock to an earlier quake that hit the Chino Hills area. Registering on the scale at 3.8, we are getting no reports of any major damage. A lot of residents are just waking up to this information," said the reporter. However, I was already up and had received a signal to "get up" before the tremor hit.

Now some may think this to be silly, but I do not. I have read and seen reports about horses and other farm animals that go into "fits of frenzy" when a major storm is approaching. Because we tune them out and do not pay attention, we miss the warning sign. As I stated before, a seismologist can track an earthquake, but he cannot accurately predict when it will happen. Believing animals serve yet another purpose, I do believe they can give us significant warning about impending danger. We know that scientists will not start using cats as predictors of weather or other natural phenomenal occurrences. And there are others who would quickly dismiss this as some chalked up notion or coincidence. All I know is that when my cats can forcefully wake me up in the middle of night seven minutes before a tremor strikes, giving me enough time to prepare myself for a quake or an aftershock, I do not take it lightly. I still believe God can use whomever He pleases to carry out a task, whether it be an angel in human form sent to deliver a message or an animal used to give a warning of impending danger. I was just grateful they "knew" what was happening and acted on it.

Reflective Thought

It is a wonderful thing to learn something new. To have your mind opened to a new idea that can spark creativity and give clarity. So often people live in a box and keep their minds closed to all the wonderful things around them. They also tend to put God in that box, placing limitations on who He is and what He can do. God, by Himself, is a creative wonder. He can do anything but fail, and we see His wonders of creation all around us. He has given us this mind to acquire knowledge. And what is knowledge? Simply put, it is information gained through experience. Once we have knowledge of a particular subject or have mastered information on a specific subject matter, we are better equipped to perform a task and execute it properly. Being made aware of anything that affects us individually or collectively can be a positive influence in our journey of life. When I learned how to drive, I was not just trying to acquire a license. I loved the idea that I could now get in a vehicle and travel wherever I wanted in a vehicle that could take me to new places where I could meet new people and have new experiences. I was made aware that there is a much bigger world out there than the lot at the DMV.

It is also my belief that animals are made aware of things that we cannot often see. It is almost as if they have insight into something we may learn later, but they can be the vehicle to transmit that information. I never frown on a dog who may bark excessively. It may be annoying to the average person, but if we look a little deeper, we may find there is a reason why he is barking. I like the story of Noah. When the flood was over, he sent a dove out to see if there was dry land anywhere. When he did this the second time, the dove came back with an olive leaf in her mouth. The dove made Noah aware that the waters had receded, and eventually they left the ark to find dry ground. Noah knew what his next course of action would be. Never underestimate where you will acquire knowledge from. It can be from a teacher, a friend, a child, and, yes, even an animal.

Chapter 15: Amina's Story

A Lesson in Sisterhood

By Dwahza Powell

"A sister can be seen as someone who is both ourselves and very much not ourselves - a special kind of double."
Toni Morrison

There are many places in the world one can dread. It can be a visit to the dentist's office or that first day in gym class where you are being taught to swim. These places can bring up our worst fears and cause us endless anxiety. Though these places may not be where many would like to visit, they are still normal activities that can become a part of our daily lives. Then there are places that no one should ever have to go or be a part of in their lifetime. These are awful places that are unsanitary, improperly maintained and, for the most part, inhumane. I am speaking of dreaded places known as puppy mills. At these large-scale commercial dog breeding operations, profit is placed above the well-being of animals. Until several years ago, many people did not know about the existence of puppy mills. When the truth about these places came out, many were horrified, all except those who saw profit over the care and welfare of an animal. Because we live in such a capitalistic society, the making of a dollar over the insensitive and inhumane treatment of dogs became more important. These places represent the dregs of society, and the eradication of them would only make for a better world. As unimaginable as these places are, the ray of hope is that something beautiful can still come forth, even in the most unlikely of pairs.

Grace was not a person given to dogs. She did not hate them, but simply had no affinity toward them. Even though they liked her, she kept her distance when it came to canines. Being from the south, she felt a dog's place was outside. Coming into the house, especially into the kitchen, was a no-no. She never really felt uncomfortable around them and actually enjoyed watching them. Still Grace possessed what all females have, a nurturing spirit. She could be drawn to someone or something and would want to make sure it was okay before she moved on. She would also make the time to check on a person that may have been in trouble and needed her help. Though she never had the desire to own a dog, she was always looking out for their best interest. Grace had built a comfortable life for herself. She was well-educated and had the sophistication and wherewithal to move through life with ease and confidence. Her career was built around helping other people in their career trajectories and making sure they were a good fit for the positions they pursued. She'd had an incredible success rate and prided herself on working with anyone, as long as they were disciplined, goal-oriented, and focused on completing a task until it was through. She was also the kind of woman who could relax and let her hair down when hanging with her girlfriends or the numerous array of friends she had made throughout the years. As Grace would put it, she felt "she had it going on."

Working with different people over the years had taken her to many different places. She was a well-traveled woman, and at this point in her career, she was comfortable settling anywhere that a solid salary could keep her in a life to which she was accustomed. She was single, smart, and enjoyed living her life. It would be during one of the high points in her career she would come across another female who would have a major impact on her life. Grace was living in New York and enjoying her career as an HR specialist. She had a contact through her job who was also a very good friend. His name was Sanchez, and he was definitely the opposite of Grace. Heriberto Sanchez was a passionate animal lover. He had owned pets all his life. As single man with one child, he loved all of his family. Within Sanchez's (as most of his friends referred to him) possession was also a beautiful German shepherd named Amina. Amina was not only a faithful companion, but a strikingly beautiful animal. She had the most wonderful coat of hair that shined in the sunlight and softly blew in the wind. Her coat was snow white and the contrast of her blue eyes made her a sight for all who gazed upon her. Amina was devoted to Sanchez and his family, as she had always felt a part of them. The other quality about Amina was that she was a purebred, and if she was to have any offspring, she would be mated with a purebred. Amina did not always understand what was happening, but she knew, at a certain point in her life, Heriberto had sent her to a place where she did not like going. It was a place that was unfamiliar to her. It was a dark place. She never understood why she was there, and her time there was always sad and painful. In her master's mind, he only wanted a litter of purebred puppies and would settle for nothing less. In Amina's mind, she felt she was being punished and did not know why.

At this dark place, there were other dogs. She was not familiar with them, but she knew she did not like them. Her behavior became somewhat aggressive in the time she was there. In all her beauty, she felt lost and unconfident. She was forced to be with other animals that she did want to be with, and sometimes the time there took a slow, painful turn. It was the hope of her master that she become impregnated and bear a litter of purebred puppies. The times that she was impregnated, her spirit was broken, and she never felt like the regal beauty she was who was to bring forth life. Amina miscarried two sets of her litter, and it was devastating to her, as it was disappointing to her human owner, but felt she was not to be with any other dog outside of that place. The only difference for Amina was that, at that place, she was monitored and allowed to come back home. Other dogs in a similar situation were not so lucky. Amina would return from that place depressed and sad. Her behavior denoted that. Sadly, her male owner did not see it. It was in the eyes of another female that Amina found some degree of solace.

While working in her office, Grace would often see Amina. Usually after Amina returned from that place, Grace always noticed something different about Amina. She did not have that proud, strong gait, and her beauty seemed to fade in the shadow of her office. She would exchange pleasantries with Sanchez, and often he would leave her there. He trusted Grace, even though she was not a dog person, but he knew Amina would be safe. Grace's heart was moved with a degree of pity on Amina. Sanchez explained to Grace what he was trying to accomplish with Amina and that she had failed again. Grace did not understand his reasoning, but could not tell him what to do with his dog. However, she could be a form of comfort for Amina, who just was not herself. Amina would look at Grace and, with sad eyes, bite down on her lips. Grace knew something had happened to her. It was something she wasn't ready to handle. She would get on the floor with Amina and look into those eyes. As they communicated in the silence between them, Grace was saying, "I'm sorry, my girl. You are in a place of pain, and I understand because I have been there before. I feel for you, and I can only stroke your beautiful coat and try to make you feel better." Amina's eyes would reply, "Why did he do this to me? I hurt, and I don't want to hurt like this anymore. What did I do wrong?" Grace, with tears in her own eyes, would say, "My female friend, you did nothing wrong. There is still love here, and in time, it shall heal the pain." Grace, in an uncharacteristic move, knelt over and embraced Amina. She felt the comfort of the human female, and let out a soft, whimpering cry.

In the days that followed, Grace became especially close to Amina. She would look forward to Sanchez bringing her by her office and hopefully getting to spend a little quality time with her. Amina's spirit would lift as she looks forward to being around Grace. They had formed an unusual bond of sisterhood that could only come about through love and kindness with a relatability factor between them. As a human female and female dog, this pair had a closeness where Grace did not want to see her newfound friend in pain anymore. Whenever Sanchez would bring her by the office, Grace would love take a break and take Amina for a walk in the nearby animal park. Amina regained her strength and her regality started to come back with every walk. Sanchez still provided for her and took care of her, as best as he could. He just never understood what was happening inside of Amina's life. She did not love him any less and never wavered in that love. It was just hard for her to embrace that situation each time she was placed there.

During one of those walks, Amina noticed another dog in the park. He was a jet-black Labrador with the silkiest coat and proudest walk. Amina was almost thirteen (in dog years) and knew that she liked this other dog she was seeing. His name was Karemu, and his owner loved him. He was a proud older gentleman named Bob. He also noticed Amina on that fateful day. As the two dogs were brought together, they did the usual smell of each other and playful romp and runaround. There was never an aggressive move by either dog, and for the first time, Amina was being herself with this other canine. It was like a refreshing breath of air on her beautiful coat. As Bob and Grace struck up a conversation, she let him know that Amina was not her dog. She also noted that she was very happy to see how much life was brought back to Amina since she had met Karemu. Grace always thought that was an unusual name for a dog, but befitting of him. He seemed happy with his name and wore it proudly. Grace told Sanchez about the relationship that was forming between Amina and Bob's dog. Sanchez was still adamant about her not cavorting with a mixed breed. Sanchez met Bob, and they were cordial and pleasant with one another. He never felt threatened by Bob and was, at least, willing to let the two animals continue seeing each other. That was the formation of the ray of hope for Amina and Karemu.

The two would begin to spend as much time as their owners would allow them together. They were always happy to see each other. Bob and Sanchez would often meet in the park. Bob got to meet Sanchez's daughter, and they formed an amiable friendship. Two men who loved their dogs had two dogs who also seemed to be falling for each other. There was never a decision to allow the two dogs to breed. Sanchez was still set on having a purebred litter. Bob was open to his dog mating with another, but never disclosed that to Sanchez. Even though Sanchez was against it, the final ruling came from Mother Nature. When actions and processes are allowed to take place naturally, the results can be beautiful. So, for the dog who was placed in a situation where she was forced to reproduce and never carried a litter to full term, it was through the meeting of a mixed breed that the natural circle of life was to continue.

Amina became pregnant with Karemu's seed. After her gestation period, she delivered a healthy litter of the most beautiful puppies. Though the dogs were eventually placed up for adoption, one puppy in the litter remained with his parents. His name was Socrates. He is a beautiful black and white mix of Labrador and shepherd with an illustrious coat. From what would be considered a dark and painful place for Amina came a beautiful love story and a healthy litter of puppies. She regained her regal stance, once again, and lived her days free and happy.

Reflective Thought

Should the truth about puppy mills be revealed to the masses, it would incite such anger and dread from those learning of its horrific practices. It is not a place that any living creation in the form of an animal should ever be exposed to. The behavior and conditions are less than humane and must be terminated. When breeders place power and avarice over the welfare of a poor, defenseless animal in such a place, they have lost their sense of humanity. Animal advocates and pet owners came to know about these places a little too late for some of our furry friends. Had we known, there would have been an all-out movement to shut these places down. And it is a place where the natural cycle of life is forced, aggravated, and abused. This was not the way God intended for animals to reproduce. The natural process of life is just that — natural. It would almost be the equivalent of me placing my own dog out with a pack of wild dogs and expecting her to defend herself. She would not survive. They would physically overpower, injure, and more than likely kill her. Dogs, like humans, when not properly socialized, can become mean, angry, and vicious. They can project this anger onto humans, as well as other dogs. We would be wise to learn more about these horrific places and do all we can to cease their practices. We can also rescue the ones who have been subjected to such places, and, hopefully, give them some modicum of wellness and happiness.

(Reflection written by Hartford Hough)

Chapter 16: I Love Mr. Buddy

A Lesson in Friendship

By Randy Ventura

"Friends are God's way of taking care of us."
Unknown

One of the most interesting aspects of owning a pet is, when you first adopt them, you will also have the opportunity to give them a name. Most animals that are in shelters and rescue adoptions centers for a long period of time are usually named by the staff. If the animal was rescued from a horrific situation, they are usually given a name by the rescuer. Just like parents with natural children look forward to naming their newborns, it can sometimes present itself as an awesome task. Some parents go back and forth for months at a time, trying to come up with the perfect name for their offspring. Most fathers feel honored to bequeath their names upon their sons. They carry the father's name with a Junior following it. In most cases, this signifies the son carrying on the legacy of the father and the family name. This has been a time-honored act within most families.

When it comes to our pets, we usually name them according to a character trait we see in them. They exude something that makes us come up with a name that is totally befitting for the animal. It is also very personal to many of us. We love giving them a name that becomes so endearing to us that we love saying it out loud often. We love it even more when our beloved animal companions learn their new name and respond to it so well. As stated before, it can be a little harder when the animal is pre-named, and we had nothing to do with it. We sort of just accept it as such. After all, it does show respect to the people who cared for the animal before they found their forever home with us. And they are probably getting used to the name, so we don't want to take it away from them. They deserve all we can give them, and if it comes to bearing that name, we just live with it. Yet sometimes a name change can come as naturally as washing your hands. It may be subtle or directly overt, but when it happens, the significance of that moment is something very special between the animal and his human companion. Such was the case of Mr. Buddy.

Randy was in Porterville, California, visiting friends. He had recently lost his wife to breast cancer and was readjusting to life and making his way through it alone. While he was with his friends, he noticed that they had a beautiful chocolate cocker spaniel by their fence. Buddy's previous owners had moved into an apartment, and Buddy was not allowed. He was left in the care of Randy's friends until he found his new forever home. Randy hadn't really given much thought to having a dog, but Buddy took a liking to him. One of the interesting aspects of their burgeoning friendship was that Buddy kept silent (which meant he was not a barker). For Randy, that was a welcome attribute since barking dogs were not his thing. He had spent the night with his friends, and he and Buddy connected. In the silence of their time together, Randy felt a connection with him.

It is here that I believe animals connect with us on a soul level. They also respond to love and care. Buddy felt that from Randy. From personal experience, I know Randy to be a loving, caring individual. He is a beautiful soul. When you meet him, there is an instant liking. I was not surprised that Buddy felt this same feeling from him. The next morning, he told his friends how much he had enjoyed Buddy and come to care for him. They smiled. Knowing for Randy that this beautiful creature would be a welcome addition to his life, they made the declaration that Buddy was going home with him, and they simply would not take no for an answer. It is always nice when others can see beautiful moments of love and connection around you that you might often miss. They knew and made preparations for Buddy to go to his new forever home with Randy.

It is amazing how the silence can communicate so greatly between two parties. Randy had often noted that Buddy did not bark, yet in his quiet, gentle manner, he spoke volumes to his now owner in his now forever home. They say the eyes are the windows to the soul, and when Randy looked into his beloved Buddy's eyes, he knew he was connecting with his animal companion on a soul level. Buddy had the most beautiful brown eyes, and with the combination of his chocolate coat (which was always well groomed), he made for a stunning creature. Randy loved his new housemate, and he began to fill the void that Randy had long missed. It gave him a sense of purpose and fulfillment. However, the fun was about to begin.

Many of us recall *I Love Lucy*, and those hilarious antics she and Ethel got into, which provided some classis comedic moments. Buddy and Randy had similar moments in their new home. Randy had just moved into a new apartment with a tiled hallway. It was here that he left Buddy, and had it gated off at the other end. When Randy would come home from work, he noticed that the dishes in the kitchen were broken where Buddy was obviously looking for something to eat. Of course, it was those puppy dog eyes that melted Randy's heart, and he could not be angry at his little furry friend. "But how did Buddy get over the fence (that was still intact when he came home)?" Buddy didn't appear to be the kind of dog who would sprint and jump, yet those dishes were broken and the kitchen was a mess. Randy decided to investigate further. One day, he appeared as if he were going out of the apartment and hid in another room. He carefully observed Buddy from that room as the seemingly sedate cocker spaniel went into action. He began his journey over the fence looking like a mountain climber just escaped from the pet store. In all his innocence, he proved to be quite agile when wanting to get over that fence and search out the hidden doggie treats. Randy watched in awe as he began his ascent and made it over the fence that was meant to block him from the rest of the apartment. Yet Buddy made it over. He knew what he wanted, and he was determined to get it. Hence the *I Love Lucy* moments because she was the same way when she wanted something, no matter how silly or foolish she looked. In her doing so, she made us laugh and it warmed our hearts. Much like Buddy. Randy could only smile in the distance at his beloved pet and then be off to the hardware store to get a more secure fence. That moment and many others they shared only brought the two closer together.

Randy felt that Buddy had carried him through some of his darkest moments, especially after having suffered such a great loss. Randy had to pick himself up and learn to walk again. Buddy, whom he now referred to as Mr. Buddy, proved to be that wonderful walking companion that he needed at that time. It really qualifies the saying that "everything happens for a reason," and God knows exactly what you need when you need it. Randy's friends saw the immediate love he had for this dog.

They knew it would be a good relationship. Randy also knew that this precious cocker spaniel had made an imprint on his life that would be forever sealed in his heart and mind. Mr. Buddy is gone now, but the love that Randy had for him has not died, and he holds his head up a little higher, and his heart is a lot stronger. Mr. Buddy is in a better place now, and because of the time and space he had on this earth, so is Randy. We love Mr. Buddy.

Reflective Thought

Friends come and go into our lives throughout our journey here. The friendship can be formed over something as simple as a cup of coffee or a social gathering. Then it can also come from a point when we are facing our darkest hour. Once the dust has settled and our hearts have healed a bit, we see there, in the clearing, a new friend. It can be a neighbor, a co-worker, and, yes, even a dog. I believe, because dogs have this incredible instinct about humans, they connect with us on a level that most humans, sometimes, miss. The depth of an emotional connection can go far between two people, and I believe that can also be experienced with animals. When we experience that connection, how special it is to have made a new friend? People forge their friendships in different ways, but as long as the person is coming from a place of sincerity and truth, you know you can open your heart to them. Animals that know love also come from that same place, and when they have found the key that unlocks your heart, let them in, because it is a good thing.

(Reflection written by Hartford Hough)

Chapter 17: The Pathway That Finds Love

A Lesson in Finding a Special Love

By Bella Quinones

"Love is like a lost object. If you search too hard, you won't find it, but if you forget about it momentarily, it will show up in the most unexpected way."
Unknown

There is no instant solution as to where you will find love. Being one of the most powerful emotions we as humans can experience, it is also the greatest force on earth. It is pretty amazing how something so powerful can be nestled in the human heart. Love is not always easy to contain. For those of us who had our first run in with puppy love or our first crush, remember how we acted. We were weepy, starry eyed and, at times, a little silly. If we had a sensible adult in our lives, we were informed that it was not the last time we would have an experience with love. It would come again. Also, if we continued to experience it on different levels, it could hurt. Now, when I speak of hurt, I do not mean an abusive hurt. I speak of a hurt where you have your first break-up or that unrequited love that may never be returned. You do find that, once you go through it, you will survive and go on. Love meets us from the beginning of our lives, and if we are so blessed, will follow us throughout till our time here is finished.

You can talk to just about anyone, and I am sure they can share a story of how their lives were changed by love. They may speak of their first boyfriend/girlfriend, their first marriage, the birth of their child, or even the purchase of their first car (some people really love their cars!). All of these experiences are valid and bear significant meaning to the individual. It also goes to show that love can be experienced in different circumstances. We may not all be on the same level, but our individual experiences with love are no less viable. Because love is so powerful, it is also varied. In this variation, love teaches us to respect. I won't look down on the person who loves his car any more than the man and woman standing at the altar to express their love by getting married. Love encompasses so many people that the pathways to love enrich and fulfill our lives. What we must do when we find love on our individual journey is embrace, cherish, develop, and, if need be, let it go. It never really leaves us because, once experienced, it remains in the treasure of our hearts.

Her name is Ziggy. She is a beautiful miniature pinscher with a lovely spotted black coat. She was in the hands of a woman who could not fully embrace taking care of this living creature because she herself was dealing with her own health crisis. Sadly, she did mistreat Ziggy with her neglect, but their journey together was to take a different path. They would be separated, but the journey Ziggy would follow was to give her and her new pet parent both a sense of fulfillment and contentment. On a trip to the vet's office to obtain medicine for her current pet, Bella happened upon Ziggy and her owner. She saw Ziggy outside the vet's office and, afterward, came in. Ziggy and her previous owner walked in shortly thereafter, and she expressed that she was going to have to let Ziggy go. She was becoming too much for her to handle, and they would have to part ways. She asked Bella if she was interested in taking Ziggy, and she was. They exchanged information. It was a decision Bella would never regret as it was to begin a new chapter in her life.

Working as a service technician, Bella was used to making fast dashes to help a customer. This was one dash she certainly did with great enthusiasm. Arriving at the home to receive Ziggy had a confrontational beginning, but quickly developed into a wonderful connection between her and her new furry companion. Bella had opened her heart to receive Ziggy, and she was there to take her to the place that would be her new forever home. The days that followed gave Bella and Ziggy time to bond. She provided her training in her new home and made Ziggy feel safe, warm, and comfortable to dry out the memories of what could've been a miserable life for her. Love always finds a way to heal. The pathway that these two were to embark on would bring great joy to their lives. Bella had gone through a rough patch in her life, and this newfound love in the form of her dog gave her a greater sense of purpose. Being a mother naturally, she knew the love of having a child. Ziggy became the "new child" that gave her another reason to wake up in the morning and live life.

Bella is a woman of strength and great determination. She is one who will fight hard for the things that are most precious in her life. Ziggy was to experience no less of what Bella gave when it came to love, understanding, patience, and kindness. She fell in love with her precious Ziggy as the days moved along. To this day, they still share a warm bond of friendship and affection that one human can have for his beloved furry companion. Ziggy stayed by her side when Bella was sick with a cold and couldn't leave the house. She provided much needed companionship and attention to her new "mommy." Bella showed that same affection and fierce care when Ziggy became ill and had a breathing attack where she almost lost her life. Bella stood on her faith and prayer for her beloved Ziggy that God would restore her breathing and they would continue on in this life. She received her blessing that day and holds gratitude in her heart that Ziggy got better.

Bella would have never thought that the day she came across Ziggy in the vet's office that their lives would be intertwined such as it is today. Their pathways in life were meant to cross, and each would bring some very needed gift to the other. Ziggy gave Bella another reason for her life here on earth. Having had experienced loss, she needed that. Bella gave Ziggy another chance at life, one that any rescue should have. A life where they matter. Ziggy had found her new forever home, a new place of love and care, after being in a place of neglect and sadness. It is a marvelous union of two souls that, though they be in different forms, still experience the power of love and all its blessed merits.

Reflective Thought

The journey of life takes us down many different paths. While we are on these pathways, we may experience the most wonderful aspect of the journey after all — love. From the moment, we are born to our present state of being, finding love during our exploits of life makes it all worthwhile. Love can come to us in many ways. The love of our parents and siblings. The love of a friend. The love of our first job. And, yes, the love of our beloved pets. Some may not understand how this human connection with a pet and the experience of love can go together. To comprehend this fact, one must look at what this experience of love means to the person receiving it. We all have different facets of our lives that the average everyday person will not see. In other words, they are not walking in your shoes and have no idea of what you are feeling, unless you express this in outward communication. They can speculate about your facet of life, but never really "get it." What one person, creature, or experience brings to your life is YOUR experience, and no one can take that away from you. The love that you feel takes place in your heart and seemingly makes all the difference in your world. When a human connects with their companion animal, the love matters to both of them because it gives them both a sense of fulfillment. Love may be complex, but it is never confused in its intent and purpose in the lives of mankind, especially as it relates to our love for our friends in the animal kingdom.

(Reflection written by Hartford Hough)

Chapter 18: Love, Inspiration and Barney

A Lesson in Inspiration and Creativity

By Laura Ambrosio-Shnitzer

"It is good to love many things, for therein lies the true strength, and whosoever loves much performs much, and can accomplish much, and what is done in love is well done."
Vincent van Gogh

Where does your inspiration come from? Does it come from your children? Nature? Faith? Wherever you receive it from most certainly changes your life and your perspective in life. You may be inspired to build something or take a trip. It may even be the creation of a school. Once that inspiration comes to you, there is concrete grounding in what you believe is possible. Inspiration is the process of being mentally stimulated to do or feel something, especially to do something creative. This definition alone sums it all up. What are you inspired to do? I believe many of us have received inspiration at some point in time within our lives. The real question then is, what did you do about it? As it is with so many people, when inspiration comes, they simply brush it off. They relish the moment for just that, a moment. Then fear, that old striking enemy, comes in. We all know in the presence of fear, you can be crippled. It will not allow you to do anything. I remember the first time I was inspired to create a wedding cake. I loved the vision I had of that cake. I wanted it to be as beautiful and special as the couple I was doing it for on their wedding day. I became excited about the possibilities and the many wonderful creative aspects I could explore when I made this cake. Then fear set in (but only for a moment). Was I good enough? Did I have enough baking experience? Would it taste as good as it was to look at? Oh, how these questions haunted me. Then something happened. I knocked fear right in the face with my hand mixer! The couple who commissioned me believed in me and my talent. Also, I believed in myself. I stood on faith, not fear. I moved forward in faith, not fear. I performed in faith, not fear. I completed the task in faith, and fear was nowhere to be found. That was a great day.

Inspiration is most definitely felt when you believe. You are not necessarily guided by an emotional trip, but something outside of yourself, and greater. It is something that settles in your heart and is accompanied by a gush of wind that acts as a confirmation. The wind is what is outside of you, and when it blows, you feel it. It moves you to the place of doing something that you may have never done before. This is where your faith takes root, and because faith is an action word, it causes you to do something. Having a lack of knowledge about something will cause you to go buy a book. Consult with an expert in the field you seek to be creative in. Spend time honing a craft that you know will one day help you create something wonderful, something that will have a greater impact in the world around you. Inspiration carries you to so many different levels that, when you are actually in the creative process, it can be mind-blowing, and, at the same time, deeply satisfying.

I do believe people can inspire other people. Have you ever been to a live show? When I was ten years old, I saw the Broadway production of *The Wiz*. I was very familiar with the original story of *The Wizard of Oz*, but this production was the soulful version of that story. Hearing Stephanie Mills sing "Home" for the first time just brought me to a whole new level of inspiration and appreciation for the creative arts. I also believe we can be inspired by our animals. We should be inspired to do something that will not only benefit them, but make a greater impression in the world. Something as simple as a dog wagging his tail signifies that he is happy. Or a cat affectionately rubbing against your leg and purring can be an inspirational factor. Animals do communicate with us in their own way, and for those of us who have really connected with our four-legged companions, the language is one all its own. Such was the case with a beautiful pit bull-beagle mix named Barney. He not only inspired his owner, but also acted as a collaborator in the process.

Laura loved animals. She had always felt a deeper connection with her pets. She was especially close to Barney. Having felt like they had traveled together in previous lifetimes, she was very in tune with his spirit. While studying in school, Laura's inspiration from Barney came in a most unusual manner. He was used to a regular time that he received dinner, except for those nights when her class kept her later. Barney, the ever-faithful dog, eagerly awaited her return home and greeted her with a wagging tail and kisses. He was happy to have her home and be back in his presence. He was also ready to eat. At school, Laura was given a project from her art and environmental class. She had to come up with a prototype that spoke to environmental awareness. It was during this regular feeding time for Barney that Laura received her inspiration. Always conscious about the environment, Laura maintained recyclable materials in her home when it came to waste management.

After taking a large bag of Barney's food and placing it in a tightly sealed container, she was about to take the empty bag outside. She was interrupted by what she felt was a thought and a vision. She thought about hundreds of pet food bags, maybe thousands, as well as some amazing fabrics. It was in that moment, while dumping out the pet food bag as refuse, that she began to form an image of a handbag. Whether it was the culmination of timing, Barney's necessity to eat, or his general spunk as her pet companion, the ideas began to flow into Laura's creative mind. Those ideas led her to develop what would become her brand of pet inspired and eco-friendly handbags. This line of products uses repurposed materials like newspapers, magazines, paintings, vintage jewelry, and even seat belts. What a marvelous idea for turning trash into treasure and sustaining the environment at the same time.

When we love our pets, as most pet owners do, we truly become their world. They are always giving back to us in so many special ways. We know of the unconditional love, but there is also the inspiration and motivation to do something truly amazing with our lives. Laura has spent countless hours volunteering at animal shelters and has been a recipient of their gratitude. It was in those moments when she saw how heartbreaking it was to leave those precious creatures and know that the local shelters did not have enough funding to maintain them all. Within her was a need to give more of herself and do something. Most pet owners go a little further, beyond their own pets, and want to do something for another animal in crisis. Barney was Laura's pride and inspiration, and she wanted to produce the means for doing something bigger than what she was already doing. Already a successful real estate agent, she was in the business of helping people purchase or sell their homes. She knew what it meant to them when they were given the keys to their first house. Knowing she was a part of that process gave her great satisfaction. She also knew that feeling when it came to animals and making sure they, too, could be placed in forever homes. Her inspiration to create a business that would produce eco-friendly bags was brilliant in itself. She has met her goal (and achieved that class project) by doing something that will help others consider the sustainability of the environment. Her feeling of "wanting to do more" also gave her a greater sense of her purpose. Knowing that the idea and inspiration came from her beloved Barney is the one thing she will carry throughout his lifetime and add to his legacy.

Reflective Thought

As we pass through life, there are so many wonderful things that can inspire us. Something as simple as a walk along the beach or a nature hike can give birth to a wonderful idea that can have a greater impact on your life and the world around you. Laura's story of inspiration came from the soul connection she had with her beloved dog Barney. It was an inspired thought that gave way to an eco-friendly business that would not only be providing a means of helping other animals in need of rescue and adoption, but also making a difference in the world that we, as humans, live also. The world has become so wasteful. If it does not benefit an individual anymore, get rid of it. That should not be the case. We can recycle and reproduce so many wonderful products that we see as trash and repurpose them for sustaining a world for now and future generations. Yes, one man's treasure can certainly become another man's treasure. Laura and her collaborator Barney found that out one night when she was simply "putting out the trash." An inspirational moment that now has new meaning and purpose for others. When we pay attention to our beloved pets, they speak to us through their actions and personality. If we are so blessed to have connected with them on a "soul" level, the possibilities of what can become are endless.

(Reflection written by Hartford Hough)

Chapter 19: A Simple Act of Compassion

A Lesson in Compassion

"It is of the Lord's mercies that we are not consumed, because his compassions fail not. They are new every morning, great is thy faithfulness."
Lamentations 3:22-23

Compassion. It is "sympathetic pity and concern for the sufferings or misfortunes of others." When we look beyond ourselves and exercise compassion, we are saying to the object of our concern, "I see you, and what you are going through. I can choose to be compassionate to your plight and have pity." When we stray from the presence of God and start to do our own thing, we often find ourselves taken over by a particular vice or some other problem that tends to lead us into troubled waters. We must realize how much we need the Lord. It is here that we see God's greatest extension of Himself and compassion toward His creation. He has pity on us when He sees that we are down and overtaken. His desire is not to see us suffer, but to console us and bring us back into a right relationship with Him.

It is not our place to judge another man or living creature's plight. That becomes the problem for many of us when we are quick to judge. We do not know the whole story. We also don't take the time to find out and listen to the story. If we did, it would probably blow many of us away. We would also probably be more motivated to do something to remedy the situation. Compassion does not judge. It also does not wait for something else to happen. It is moved upon by the heart. If your heart desires to be like the heart of God, then compassion will take you further into any situation and cause you to do more than you thought you could. As in the story of the Good Samaritan, the Levite and the priest passed by the man who had been robbed and beaten. They ignored him completely. The Samaritan stopped, placed bandages on his wounds with oil and wine, and placed him on his donkey and took him to a nearby inn. He paid for all his expenses and told the innkeeper when he passed that way the next day, he would reimburse him any more expenses incurred. Jesus told us to "go and do likewise."

I saw this action within myself and how I extended it to a beloved cat of mine. I first met Belvedere when I was working for a hotel in North Hollywood, California. A co-worker of mine knew I had a cat and had some experience with them. I really could not take on another animal and didn't want to push the envelope with my building's management. When I first saw him, I was struck by his beautiful golden coat and those mesmerizing green eyes. Unbeknownst to me, this pitiful creature had a lot more issues than I could see with the naked eye. My heart was moved by him, and I knew he could not go to the shelter because they were overrun with animals and his days would have been numbered. I went against caution and took him in. He was infested with fleas, had conjunctivitis, and had not been vaccinated. He was also very shy and withdrawn. I had to quarantine him from my other cat (Guffy) until he received proper medical attention. My compassion for him was so strong that I made sure he received all the necessary medical attention, and I did not care about the cost. I wanted him well and did not want his misfortune as an animal to be this way. He needed love and understanding. Compassion drew that out of me. It was this same feeling when I come across a homeless person. I feel terrible about their situation, but there is something inside of me that wants a better way of life for this individual. Ultimately, they must make that choice as to where they want their life to go. In the case of Belvedere, he had no choice.

What could have brought him to this stage in his life? Was his former owner not caring enough to see that he was in need? What were the circumstances surrounding him that brought him to that moment where he met me? I am a believer that all things happen for a reason. There are no mistakes in God or His plan for mankind. God knew that I would have the heart to care for this beautiful creature. He knew that compassion would overtake me to the point where something had to be done. He would also make a way to see that everything that was to happen for Belvedere, from that point, would be executed to the fullest. I was especially happy when the lady who brought him to us received all the medication he needed those first few weeks. That would have been a costly undertaking, but a way was made. Everything from that point fell on me. I just knew that compassion was still ruling my heart, and I was going to make sure that this precious cat received all that he needed to get him back to optimum health.

After living with us for a few months, Belvedere regained his health, became acclimated to his new environment, and came out of his shell to receive the love, warmth, and attention my other cat and I gave to him. He was the recipient of compassion, and when it was received, he was one of the most endearing, lovable creatures I had ever encountered. He knew that someone cared for him, and in return, he gave that love to other animals and humans. He still maintained a shy side but was still a bundle of love. It was such an amazing transformation to watch this pitiful creature, who could have been at death's door, respond to the hand of compassion given to him. His response was beautiful and, to this day, will always hold a place in my heart as my lovable Poo-Boo.

The arm of compassion had been extended to Belvedere so many times in his short life with us. He was always dealing with something that made me have to watch over him all the more. No parent wants to see any of their children sick. I certainly did not want to see this beloved creature in pain. There were times I would look at him and see how happy he was to have been embraced by love. I often said it was patience, kindness, and love that healed him. It drew him out of his shell, and he responded to the love that was surrounding him. I hated to think he may have been abused. So often, it could be the case of a former owner who becomes ill, and their beloved creature is left behind. Maybe he wandered away from the place that he knew as home and became lost. He may have had to survive on his own until he found his new forever home. Whatever the situation, love found its way to him, and it healed him. I still miss that morning nuzzle when he would jump on my bed and wake me up. My "fuzzy alarm clock" has not rung for a while now. I carry his memory in my heart forever knowing the compassion I extended to him that day made a difference in his life.

Reflective Thought

We have all seen someone down on their luck or in a place where life may have dealt them a hard hand. It is not easy to watch another human being drug through the mire of misfortune. No matter what reason brought them there, they should not have to stay there. It would take the heart of one who realizes that "there but for the grace of God go I." Compassion opens the heart of a man to feel sorrow and pity for another man's plight. It also reaches out to help someone. Everyone can extend compassion in some way, shape, or form. I had the opportunity to take in a poor, helpless creature who was in desperate need of tender, loving care. Others can share their resources or even offer that person a meal. Compassion can also be as simple as a smile or a hug. How you extend this form of God's love may be the only beacon a person sees in the course of a day. Keep your heart open to the flow of compassion because, when it touches your heart, it can make a world of difference in another living creature's life.

Chapter 20: Two Hearts

A Lesson in the Affairs of the Heart

By Victoria Stewart

"The best and most beautiful things in the world cannot be seen or even touched - they must be felt with the heart."
Helen Keller

What is it about the depth of the human heart? It seems to go into places unimaginable, yet when it reaches its destination, it is still felt on a very emotional and real level. Often the heart goes a painful journey that can reduce a person to their knees. Then there are those times when it reaches points of pleasure that can bring an almost endless degree of happiness. It is this journey of the heart that carries all of us through its twists and turns, yet we still seem to enjoy the ride. We come back for more, as if the next place our heart takes us will bring a sweeter outcome, or so we hope. It is this journey where two people can find love on a level that some never seem to reach. Each journey takes a person somewhere. Oftentimes, we are simply a casual observer to the outcome of the journey for two people. We watch them laugh, cry, and share moments that testify to the affairs of the heart. It is a beautiful sight to watch two people in love. It makes you appreciate the process they have been through, and you know it will carry them as far as they want to go. When this love is intertwined with another creature, there appears to be the most amazing connection that becomes obvious to everyone who sees it.

There is also the frailty of the heart when the connection seems to be lost. A person can wander around aimlessly when their heart seems to have lost what gave it purpose and life. This, of course, can be said of our connection to God. When we seem to stray from the source that gave us life, there is a sad disconnect as one goes through the human experience. The incredible testament to His power is how He will use anyone or anything to cause our hearts to get back in alignment with Him. How glorious is the moment when the heart feels reconnected to its source of energy, vitality, and inspiration? The journey of the heart can be felt between the most unlikely of pairs. When the two are together, it can be astounding. And when the two are apart, it can be an astonishing event. This was the case between my auntie Pee-Wee and her beloved cat, Cleveland.

Auntie Pee-Wee was not my biological aunt. It is an interesting dynamic when two families can become so close that bloodlines are not even recognized. The Allens and the McBrides were bonded through our grandmothers. The two women, Irma Allen and Annie Lou McBride, were so close that anyone who saw them would automatically think they were sisters. They were both from the south, and they were kind, loving, God-fearing women who raised their children to love God, their fellow man, and each other. Hailing from the south, there was always a sense of love, family, and faith. The two women made sure their children knew God and did not stray from the principles in His word. The bond between the grandmothers carried over to their children, grandchildren, and great-grandchildren. Ms. Irma and Mother McBride had sons and daughters of their own, so it became very natural for us to refer to one another as "auntie" or "cousin." There was not the slightest sense that we were not blood related because, no matter the time or place, we were always family. This loving characteristic was especially noticeable in Auntie Pee-Wee. She was Ms. Irma's middle daughter. She had the sweetest personality and demeanor that I ever noticed in a woman outside of the ones in my own family. She was kind, gentle, and had the softest spot for animals. I knew it was on that level that we had an instant connection. Other members of the family loved animals, too, but there were always constraints and issues. Auntie Pee-Wee never had a problem finding an animal and taking it under her wing. She had two natural children of her own, and she raised them to always be kind to animals. It was understood that these creatures were God's gift to the world and should be treated as such. The children never really understood the death of an animal for Auntie Pee-Wee would shield it from them until they were old enough to understand. Smart as they are, they pretty much figured out what had happened and accepted it as a part of the life cycle. Their love and concern for animals carries on to this day.

When Auntie Pee-Wee found Cleveland, it was on Linden Boulevard in Brooklyn. He was a stray kitten that surely would have died had she not rescued him. It was her maternal instincts that caused her to take the little brown tabby home. She came to love Cleveland as her "new child" and was as protective and caring of him as any mother would be. Her own kids accepted the latest "addition" to the family as natural and normal. They knew their mother, and it was no surprise to them when she undertook such a task as to raise and care for another animal. Cleveland was no ordinary cat, however, and the family was soon to find out what made him so special and endearing to their mother.

They watched him as he grew and became their mother's shadow. There was not a room Auntie Pee-Wee could not find herself in and Cleveland not be in it. It was sweet to watch him follow her around the house like a child who would not let his mother's hand go. As he got older, Auntie Pee-Wee spoke to him as naturally as she did her own kids. She still maintained a full-time job and, oftentimes, had to break the "Cleveland cycle" just to get out of the house and go to work. As with most people, Auntie Pee-Wee had a morning routine as she readied herself for work. Cleveland was always somewhere nearby, watching and waiting. He never wanted her to leave him in the house, but knew that, during certain parts of the day, she would be gone for several hours. He became so acquainted with her routine that he even tried to sabotage her for leaving him for so long. Though she always expressed her love for him and let him know that she would be back later in the day, he simply did not want her to go. As if knowing what can really get under a woman's skin, Cleveland would snare Auntie Pee-Wee's stockings because he knew she would have to come back for another pair, and he got to keep her a few minutes longer. Noticed by her children as they were getting ready for school themselves, they would find endless humor in watching their mother play this back and forth run in (no pun intended) with Cleveland and the stockings. Auntie Pee-Wee's son even noticed that Cleveland almost had a Cheshire cat grin on his face as his mother faced yet another bout with Cleveland.

In the evening, when things had settled and all was well in their home again, Auntie PeeWee would be in the kitchen preparing supper, and Cleveland would come into the room and perch himself on the step ladder and watch her. He wasn't just watching her; he was studying her. She was well acquainted with his mannerisms, and he wanted to be the same with her. It was obvious to a casual observer that Cleveland loved my auntie Pee-Wee and would do anything to remain in her presence. Auntie Pee-Wee's daughter, Renee, had even noticed, when she would go in to the kitchen and try to talk to Cleveland, he would "shoo" her away with his paw and go into the other room to be with her mother. Renee wasn't rattled by this. She knew how devoted Cleveland was to her mother. Cleveland accepted them as members of the family, but always had that special affinity toward Auntie Pee-Wee.

I can recall, as I got older and went away to school, my little routine when I came home for a semester break or extended weekend was to visit the Allens. I knew we would all gather in church on Sunday, but I liked to make a personal visit to their homes and catch up on things. I would always end up staying at Mother McBride's house, but had to make a few stops along the way. It always began with a visit to Ms. Irma, who was just as endearing and sweet as I always knew her to be. I liked stopping by because we would have good talks, and she always had some delicious cake. Also living in the Kingsborough projects were my niece and her husband. I would go sit with them for a while and enjoyed the visit. Then I made my way to Starrett City to Mother McBride's home. After Papa McBride had passed, she downsized to a small but comfortable apartment. It was a good location for her, and she was still close to family, including Auntie Pee-Wee and Auntie Betty, who both lived right across the street. After stopping at Mama's house, I would always make my way to see Auntie Pee-Wee's. Still as sweet and kind as I knew her to be, it was always a welcome call to her house. And in the midst of this visit, there was Cleveland. Still the ever-devoted cat who loved my auntie and remained by her side. He was always friendly with me (maybe because he knew I would only be there for a short while). I also noted how Auntie Pee-Wee doted on her little Cleveland.

A few years later, Auntie Pee-Wee took ill. She did not want to reveal to the family what was happening with her medically because she would rather not have the family worry. Her illness was more aggressive than we, as the family, could have known. We just kept her in our prayers and hoped for the best outcome. While she was home, Cleveland stayed by her side constantly. He became her vigilant companion. Auntie Pee-Wee was also very private, so many of us did not really know how ill she had become. We did not flood the house with visitors but relied on constant communication through her children and sisters. Renee was deeply concerned about her mother but also wondered about Cleveland. He could not speak to her, but she knew he was in tune with the woman who had been his constant companion since he was a kitten. He loved this woman and, though he could not say it, did not want her to go anywhere. After a while, her illness became such that she had to be hospitalized. Renee was now even more concerned for Cleveland because her mother was not in the house. Cleveland maintained a constant vigil on her bed. He would walk around the house looking for her, hopefully awaiting her return through the door. But it was not meant to be. It came to pass that Auntie PeeWee succumbed to her illness, and the family rallied around each other, as another soldier made her final transition. Auntie had lived a good life, was a good wife and mother, and a loving sister, friend and, more than what other eyes did not see, a faithful companion to a small rescue named Cleveland. After the funeral, Renee took Cleveland to another family member's house. She knew it would be a difficult period, and with family and friends coming through, she did not want Cleveland to stress. Five days later, Cleveland came back home. As always, he roamed the house, looking for Auntie Pee-Wee.

How do you explain to a cat that his best friend is gone? He stayed on her bed, but it was evident, his spirit was losing heart. He had lost energy and the personality that was so endearing was fading. Even though we could not talk to Cleveland in his language, he knew. Exactly one week after Auntie Pee-Wee had made her transition, Renee came home. She had started moving forward with her life and the process of losing her mother. She called out to Cleveland to come, but no response. She figured he was still in her mother's room, so she went in to look after him. To her dismay, she found Cleveland curled up in her mother's bed; he had quietly passed. Cleveland had not been sick or shown any sign of illness. In her grief, Renee knew what had happened. She had just lost her mother, and now, another member of her family was gone, and not from any normal condition that could be diagnosed. He had simply passed away from a broken heart.

The two hearts that were joined in this life were now together again. These two wonderful lives had made a connection here on earth, and the love they had for each other would carry them through eternity. Auntie Pee-Wee and Cleveland are missed. They are thought of in the fondest way, with bright memories and an incomparable friendship. Two hearts were joined in a most unusual fashion and on the most unique of journeys. To those of us who observed from the outside, we saw a beautiful love story played out before our very eyes.

Reflective Thought

There is a scripture that says, "The heart is more deceitful than anything else. It is incurable bad. Who can understand it." Jeremiah 17:9 (HCSB version). With all its complexities and often misunderstood state, who really can know the heart but

God? The heart can fool you. It can cause you to think things that simply are not meant to be. It can also hurt, but, in time, find healing. When it comes to two hearts experiencing this life journey through humankind, one has to take a closer examination at its core. The depth of love that one person can feel for another can go so deep and be so connected that it would seem the pair were made for each other and walk hand in hand. I saw this in my great-uncle and great-aunt. They had been married over sixty years. In their final years, when their health was fading, they had been separated through hospitalization. My uncle passed first, and then one week later, my aunt made her transition. They loved each other so much, and the thought of being worlds apart was too much for their hearts to bear. It can also be said of the relationship between man and animal. The connection of two hearts can be so profound and reach a level that many will not even begin to understand. Though the heart may be considered deceitful, it can also feel abundant fulfillment when connected to the right source. This emotional depth is reached by the most important of creatures. The two hearts involved.

(Reflection written by Hartford Hough)

Chapter 21: Being a Part of Something Great

A Lesson in Value

"The greatness of a nation and its moral progress can be judged by the way its animals are treated."
Mahatma Gandhi

If you are a citizen of the United States, you have said, at one point in time, that you live in a great country. Whether you were born here and have enjoyed the benefits of being a part of this great land or you came here as an immigrant and you are pursuing the American dream. Living in this country has many merits. And there are so many things that make this country what it is and add to its greatness. From the diversity that has encompassed us to the appreciation of our differences. People around the world look at us as an example of what being a part of a great nation means. They look at how people are treated. The opportunities given to them and their families. The freedoms we so often take for granted. And they also watch the smaller acts, no less significant, but closely examined. How we treat those who are too defenseless to care for themselves. The homeless, the outcasts, the downtrodden, the poor, and our animals.

One probably would not consider this of great importance. Should a nation be judged by the way they treat animals? Yes. Animals would fall into the category of the defenseless among us. No matter how you may view it, when an animal is born, like a child, it is helpless and needs someone to care for it. Nature has shown us that, when animals are born, their mothers care for them in their tender and fragile state. Instinctual and steadfast, a mother will care for her offspring until they are able to go out on their own. In the wild, a mother bear does not read a book on how to care for her cubs. She knows what to do and does it. In a more domesticated setting, the same principle applies when animals are cared for in a safe and secure environment. Dogs, cats, and hamsters are instinctually equipped to handle their own. Yet there are those animals who do not have this privilege. They may be referred to as "feral" animals. Their presence is no less important among us.

What it really comes down to is what we value. Some people do value things more than they do people. Personally, I think that is sad. We cannot expect everyone to be as enthusiastic about a passion we may have or a project we may be working on. It would be the hope that common human decency would rule the day and the things that we value are esteemed in a much better light. I knew someone who seemed to value his automobile more than the care of his wife. She was dealing with health issues in her later years, and it would have been nice for him to run her to the doctor's office or even take her out for a nice drive in the country. This was too much because it would have gotten his car dirty on a day when he just washed it. Ironic thing was he placed so much value in that car that karma found him out. His wife had passed away, and he became ill in his later years.

While he was laid up trying to get back to better health, his car just sat in the yard, gathering dust and dirt until it was no good. Placing value on a human life will carry you much further in this life than placing hollow value on a vehicle. You can always replace a car. A human life, you cannot.

I had a recent experience where I came across a deceased possum. It is never easy to come upon a dead animal and not have some kind of reaction. I looked at this creature, and it had obviously been poisoned. There were no visible signs of trauma on the animal's body. Actually, it had the most beautiful coat of hair. At first, I was cautious about going near it because I thought he might be playing "possum." If this creature had jumped up at me after that, I would have been in the next county in five seconds flat! Yet he did not move, and it was determined he was dead. I asked a neighbor about the creature, and he seemed to know nothing. For that matter, he really couldn't care less as he tended to his shed and fixing some contraption. I did not want to see this creature become plain "roadkill" right here in my neighborhood. I called animal control, and because it was a holiday, they could not send someone out to claim the animal. So I went into "animal control" mode myself. I secured the area and set up some cones on the street. Most drivers who see a dead animal in the street will try swerving their cars to avoid hitting the animal. Others, who couldn't care less, will roll over the creature with no regard. I am of the mindset that, just as in life, a living creature should be treated with dignity and respect, even if it has passed on. If it were a human, we would be out of our cars, on our cell phones, attempting to flag down anyone who could help us. Why should an animal whose life has expired be treated any different?

A general poll of the average American asked the following question: What do you value the most? The top two answers were their life and their family. These are valid responses, and both have merit in their content. Other responses included money, relationships, careers, and friends. All very good answers. The top two can be examined a little closely. If you say you value your life, then that means all life should be important to you. That means it has worth. So how is it that, if we say we value life, should the life of an animal (any animal) be considered less? Again, I don't expect everyone to run down and join their local chapter of the ASPCA. This is just to make us (as humans) a little more aware of these precious lives that we see all the time. They may not be in your possession, but it is still a valuable life. One thing I can appreciate is the K-9 unit of law enforcement. When a dog is trained to work in highly specialized situations, his life is regarded as very important by his partner, the department, and the entire force. If he should die in the line of duty, he is honored just as any officer would be, with dignity and respect. I like that.

The other answer was family. Who among us that owns a pet does not regard this creature as a member of our family? Because we value our family, it begs the question — how far would we go to help out our family? For many, the answer would be obvious. They would go to the ends of the earth to help or save a member of their family. Does this devalue our four-legged friends, if a crisis comes upon us? I recall calling into this radio show one night. The topic was "Should landlords charge extra for pet rent?" The radio host, who was quite hilarious in his own right, felt they should not. I understood why landlords would charge. I have seen what some people do to an apartment when they leave. It is really bad sometimes when they have a pet. Not all pet owners are like this. The host then transitioned into what would happen if they decided not to rent to you at all. I replied, "I guess me and my animals will be on a park bench somewhere because we are a package deal. You don't want to rent to me? Somebody else will." The host then chimed in because he loved his dogs so much. "I guess I will be out there with you, my friend, and we will all roast marshmallows!" I cracked up at his response.

Though we laughed, I understood where he was coming from with his answer. What value do we place on our pets? Our nation is constantly being watched and scrutinized for how we treat one another. I understand Gandhi's statement about our "moral progress" being judged by the way we treat our animals. In other words, the least among us. We must always be mindful of the poor, the helpless, the weak, and the downtrodden. It is sad but true, animals also fall into these categories of living. Thank God there are groups and organizations dedicated to helping them out and tending to their well-being, giving them a chance at a renewed life and the opportunity for us to be better people, yes, better human beings.

Reflective Thought

We do live in a great nation. It seems as if what we've come to value has waned in the past few years. We have lost that sense of worth and importance for all of God's living creatures. We have replaced it with worthless, materialistic things that will eventually fade. Things that can be replaced. We must restart the emphasis on what is really important in our country (and in the world, for that matter). We must place value where it really counts. Our families are definitely a good place to start. It seems the family has been under attack lately. We might focus on the good of our families, strengthen the bonds, and continue to build legacies for future generations. I will always regard my animals as "members of my family." As long as I have family, they will be a part of it. We must also see the value in an animal's life, just as we do in that of a human. We must refasten that tie of human decency and look out for the "less among us." As human beings, we are so much better than the way things are often portrayed in the newspapers and social media. Let's rise up to the occasion and look out for one another, where care and concern are not virtues of the past. Let them be very present and constant guides for a better tomorrow.

Chapter 22: I am Going to Make It Out

A Lesson in Determination

By Robin Sierra

"You may encounter many defeats, but you must not be defeated. In fact, it may be necessary to encounter the defeats, so you can know who you are, what you can rise from, how you can still come out of it."
Maya Angelou

How much of a fight do you have in you? In pursuing a goal, you will come up against deterrents and hurdles that will truly bring out the fight in you. This would seem an interesting point to analyze because we don't often equate fighting with the pursuit of a goal. We just do what we have to do in order to reach it, but there will be some moments when you have to "fight" through some things to get there. For the runner, he has to fight through the grueling training schedule that will allow them to compete in their race and, hopefully, become the champion. For the student, he will have to fight through long nights of study, tiredness, and, yes, procrastination in order to reach his goal of finishing the class and eventually graduating. To the business person, in order for her to reach the goal of becoming CEO, she must fight through moments of sexism, disrespect, and hardships in order to reach the top position. Her fight will not be in an arena, but in the corporate boardroom and office setting where she is told to maintain her place, for women do not belong at the executive level of the business. That fight was started and put in its place many years ago by women who were determined to fight through and pave the way for others. These fights are critical because they really bring out what is in you. The one characteristic that shines throughout this "fight" is something known as determination.

Determination is a resolution to complete what has been started. It is knowing why you are doing what you are doing and finding the stamina and strength to go through all the way till the end. What if the obstacles seem insurmountable? I am reminded of this drive and determination from one of my favorite stories, *The Lord of the Rings*. In the story, Frodo and Sam, who were hobbits, had to take the ring of power back to Gondor and throw it in the Mount of Doom. This would destroy its power and bring order back to the world as they knew it. If you are familiar with the story, you know that the odds were truly stacked against these two hobbits. From the outset, it looked as if their mission was impossible and they would not complete the task given to them. The one thing these two had was determination. It was determination of the heart that drove them into the precarious adventures and overwhelming enemies that sought to bring their demise. Yet, they persevered and pressed on until they reached their destination. And when it seemed like they were at death's door, the hope that remained faithful to them, brought them back home to safety with family and friends. This kind of determination was also displayed by the dog Snowy. Her story was one that would pit a dog against many odds, yet she was determined to overcome them all and find her loving, forever home.

On the beautiful island of Hawaii, Robin Sierra could see the volcano from the sea. Against the black night sky, there was an orange glow. The next day, she ventured to the volcano to witness its magnificence. The name of the volcano was Kilauea. She came upon the place where the volcano met the ocean. This volcano had been steadily erupting for thirteen years. The lava had been moving so slowly that she was able to stand at the leading edge and watch. Fire spilled into the water, hissing and churning, creating white clouds of boiling steam into the air. She came as close as the intense heat would allow. The pace of this lava was deceptive. Nothing stood in its way, not stop signs, not trees, nor whole towns. There was a siege by the U.S. Army when the lava was threatening to destroy homes. They tried to divert its path, with dubious success, by dropping 600-pound bombs in its path. Diversion was the best they could do. Nothing could stop the lava from reaching its destination. Robin was impressed. She wanted to be just like that, determined and unstoppable.

One day, a little white dog showed up at Robin's back door. She lay under a mesquite tree, quite scraggly and with little cactus spines in her fur. Her ribs protruded like xylophones through her dull and worn coat. After weeks of these daily visits, Robin could no longer bear to watch this poor creature sit out in the Sonoran Desert heat. She allowed her to come inside, where she could cool off and refresh herself with water. On this fateful day, Robin just happened to be reading about the volcano Kilauea. According to Hawaiian legend, there was a goddess, Pele, who resided in the volcano and appeared to mortals in one of three forms: a beautiful young chieftess, an elderly woman, or a little white dog.

Robin began investigating around the neighborhood and found out that the dog's name was Snowy. She was never allowed in the house. She slept on the concrete patio and usually escaped from her yard minutes after everyone in the family left for work or school. Robin worked from home. It was soon discovered that Snowy preferred staying at her house, where she would have some company. When her owners found out, they went to great lengths to keep Snowy restrained. Yet, she continued to show up at Robin's house for her visits, undaunted. Snowy had tunneled out under the fence and had made her way on the other side. Her owners tied her to a tree, where she barked and howled all night long. She broke free of the collar. One day, Robin took her back home. She led her into the gate and watched as Snowy did something astounding. She positioned herself and leapt, scaling the seven-foot, slatted wooden fence. She was poised on the narrow ledge like a tightrope walker, looking for a place to jump down where she wouldn't land on the ubiquitous and spiny prickly pear.

The family who owned Snowy brought home another dog, thinking the companionship might be the key to keeping her home, but Snowy wanted no part of this intruder and continued her breakouts. They tied an empty plastic gallon milk container to her collar, which was intended to keep her from crawling under the fence. One day, Robin came home from a walk and heard a strange sound. Because she had accidentally left the front door ajar, Snowy had come in and was clattering around the house, milk container trailing behind her and banging against the clay tile floor. The neighbors' final attempt was to confine her to a harness, a contraption of half a dozen black nylon straps and buckles that looked like some medieval torture device and was designed to restrict her movement, to keep her from jumping. But this wrath-like Houdini did it again, appearing in Robin's living room, straps flying, tail wagging. Robin was impressed.

Robin eventually worked out an agreement with the neighbors. When the youngest son would leave for school in the morning, he would drop Snowy off at her house and then pick her up in the evening. After a month went by, Robin could no longer bear sending her back there again. Finally, she asked them if she could have Snowy. They agreed, and Snowy moved in with Robin. She gave her a diet of millet and hamburger, vitamins, and flax seed oil. Snowy was loved and fawned over day and night, and given daily walks in the wilderness. She had full reign of the house with, at least, eight places to sleep. She gained weight, and instead of being scraggly and anxious, she became content and beautiful.

It was clear to Robin why this dog was in her life. Like the volcano, she was the essence of determination and, by example, demonstrated to her that she could conjure up a fierce tenacity when she had her heart set on doing something, even when it seemed insurmountable.

Reflective Thought

Determination at its best moments is an affirmation to an individual that when they are looking at mountain top barriers, they can still make it to the top and over the mountain. Such was the case of Sir Edmund Hilary and Tenzing Norgay. They were the first two men to reach the summit of Mount Everest. Considering the steepness of this mountain, the rough terrain, and the weather conditions, one might attempt to go but so far before retreating to the base of the mountain. Hillary and Norgay were a part of an expedition. Some from the expedition told them to retreat and forego the climb. Determination won the order of the day when, against all the odds, he and his friend reached the summit within minutes of each other. This is where determination plays a vital role in the life of a person. You can make it through any situation that you place your heart and mind to do. You will be beset with obstacles as par for the course, but nonetheless, you must press through and press on. It will be that "press in the push" that will allow you to see the finished goal. You will conjure up that tenacity, just as Snowy did. No matter what you put in my way, on my person, or through my course, I am determined to make it through these obstacles and come out a winner.

(Reflection written by Hartford Hough)

Chapter 23: We Have to Get Along

A Lesson in Cooperation

"When times are tough and people are frustrated and angry and hurting and uncertain, the politics of constant conflict may be good, but what is good politics does not necessarily work in the real world. What works in the real world is cooperation."
William J. Clinton

"We have to go along to get along" has been quoted many times in the past few years. The world in which we live has become one of uncertainty and, yes, civil unrest. Gone are the days when we used to look out for one another and there was a spirit of cooperation that governed our families, our communities, and our lives. In 1991, the world witnessed the horrific beating of a young African-American male named Rodney King. This brutal beating sparked outrage within communities around the nation and protests from around the world when the footage of that beating was released. The days that followed were ones of civil unrest and violence. The situation only increased as the officers who were charged in the beating of King were acquitted. It began days of brutal attacks, violence, and anger. People carried this anger to work, school, and even to church. It seemed, for a time, our nation was truly divided. It was during the riots that King appeared before the media and tried to quell the situation at large. He became widely known for saying, "Can't we all just get along?" Though there were many who thought him to be foolish for saying this, there was significant truth in Rodney King's words. Had the spirit of cooperation truly died?

From a personal standpoint, I do not necessarily agree with the saying, "You have to go along to get along," because I do have a mind of my own, and if I don't agree with something, I am not going to follow the crowd just to get along with the crowd. However, I do believe we can "get along" with some degree of amicable behavior and respect. The cooperative spirit does not seek an outcome of hatred or anger. It definitely does not promote violence where there is bloodshed and pain. Cooperation is a "process of working together to a mutual end." I believe it can be said that most, if not all, people would like to see peace in the world. We know of many advocates and groups that promote peace through marches, demonstrations, concerts, and programs, all in an effort to promote peace. In order for us to achieve such a goal, we must work together. In coming together and sharing thoughts and ideas, we can all bring something to the table, and hopefully work toward achieving this goal. Peace will never be reached on a large scale if it is not first achieved on the smallest, hardest scale — within ourselves. I am so often brought back to this very needed lesson, and I have to keep myself in check, even when the lesson is brought back to my remembrance by the smallest of creatures, my dog Ginger.

By most standards, Ginger would be considered a very well-traveled little canine. She has accompanied me on numerous trips and vacations and was just as at ease about traveling as I had ever seen a dog. I can always appreciate having her with me because, over the years, my love for flying has taken a backseat to the pleasure I once had when it came to making travel plans. Having once worked for the airline industry, I used to adore getting on planes and zipping off to another city that was not my own and flying at incredible speed that brought me from one destination to the next in record time. When I was an employee, one of the benefits was flying anywhere we wanted to for a very reduced rate and on standby. More times than not, there was always a seat available, and my bags and I were ready to go. This all seemed to change after 9/11 happened. It not only changed our world, but also my love for jet-setting in the air. I had to be reminded that it was still "the safest way to travel," and come back to the appreciation for what is meant in my travel itinerary. When Ginger came onto the scene, she brought a lesson of her own that would take me back to the beginning, and also refresh my understanding of what cooperation meant.

John F. Kennedy International Airport is one of the largest and busiest airports in the world. The number of travelers and employees keep the place moving at record speed with its bustling crowds, travel groups, stores, restaurants, and other establishments that lend to its appeal. With over 37,000 employees and a new Air-Tran system that connects to all the major transportations hubs to and from the city, the airport garners millions of travelers per year through its busy door. Since 9/11, there has been a significant increase in airport and travel security. It is on this note that I must admit I have not been a happy camper when it comes to travel through this or any other major airport. Now, don't get me wrong because I am all for security and precaution, but everything from the check-in to the TSA screening and final gate check, I had not realized how easy (and good) we had it before. We were traveling from New York back to California, and all I wanted to do was get to my seat on the plane and rest for the next five and a half hours.

On this particular day, that was not going to happen. So, when it came to cooperating with the officials at the airport, I was about to be tried to no end.

Ginger and I had arrived in plenty of time for our flight. I even had more than enough time to take her out to the pet relief area. She handled herself, and then we were ready to go. Or so I thought. She was definitely readier than me. We came into the check-in area, and fortunately there was no crowd on my particular airline. At this point, Ginger may have had to get on the scale to make sure she was within the weight requirement. Her diet as of late hadn't been good, and I was expecting the agent to hit me with an excess fee. He was merciful and kind, and she passed the test (barely), but we found favor. Because Ginger was registered as an ESA (Emotional Support Animal), I was able to walk her freely through the airport, provided I keep her on her leash. We were then off to our favorite part of the journey, the TSA screening. It was here you had to practically get naked just to get through the screener. On this trip, I thought I was well-traveled enough to know what would set that machine off and what would not. I guess I was wrong. However, I wanted to remain in the spirit of cooperation and not let anything rattle me here. Ginger was off her leash, and I had removed her harness which would have surely gone off. It was here that Ginger took center stage to everyone's attention, watching and waiting for me. On this particular day, this agent seemed to want me to strip down to nothing just to get through that metal detector. I stepped through the door three times, and three times it went off. I thought I had moved every metal object from my being, yet that buzzer kept going off. Ginger sat there and watched me. She could tell I was getting frustrated, and walked over to the machine. You would have thought she was going to steal something as they went into tactical alert. She simply walked over to the machine to make sure I was keeping it cool. She looked at me with those adorable brown eyes as if to say, "Now listen, we have to get on this flight. Give them whatever they want and keep it together. You will be all right and so will they as long as you cooperate with them. I know you, and don't let your mouth get you into trouble." I nodded at her and smiled. I went through the screener once again, and of course, it went off. I was then asked to step to the side, so they could search me with that metal wand. I was frustrated at this point because I do not like when I have to take off my shoes, my belt, all the contents on my person, my carry-on, and place them in those individual buckets. Plus, I had all of her things and her carrier. Ginger daintily walked over to the other side, sat down, and waited for me. I knew I had to keep it cool because they did not need a frustrated black man to go off because of all these "search details." Ginger sat up and looked at me again. "Steady, man. We are almost there" was the read on her face. I simply could not lose it for her or myself. She walked over to me again, and I could tell she was through with all this searching. This time, she looked at the TSA agents as if to say, "Can this be over with? I want to get on this plane, crawl under the seat, and get my nap. You all are taking too long, and he is really not having it." That's my girl!

Then, I was summoned by another agent because he had to search my computer bag. At this point, I was done. I had my shoes and belt off and was praying that my pants didn't fall down, and now I had to go through another search. I did not want to respond to him until all my things had come through the scanner and I had gathered my personal belongings. I had to see what he was doing with my computer and what prompted this new search. After what seemed an endless process, I finally grabbed up all my things and proceeded to the nearest seat to gather myself. I felt like I had been through a car wash, and I wasn't even clean. Fortunately, we still had time before our flight left, but I was sitting there, totally undone. Ginger sat in front of me. I have learned to read what is in her eyes so clearly. "I'm sorry you had to go through that. Now get yourself together, and let's get on this plane." I chuckled to myself when I sensed that reading. I did get it together, gathered up all of our things, and proceeded toward our gate. I grabbed something to eat from one of the vending kiosks and said I would eat before I boarded the plane. It was at this time I realized my gold ring was missing. I frantically searched myself, hoping it would be in my pocket. It was not. Then it hit me. I knew exactly where it had been misplaced ... during that search and seizure from the TSA screening. It was in one of those plastic bins where you have to remove all your jewelry and metal pieces. Because I had become so frustrated by the screening, it was not picked up when I graciously tried to get all my things and get away from those people. I was about to go back to that gate and search out my ring, when Ginger looked up at me with those Maltese-terrier eyes and said, "Don't even think about it. You can get another ring. You cooperated with those people, did what you had to do, and you moved on. What's a little collateral loss?" I smiled at her in agreement because I knew she was right. It was at that time that they began pre-boarding for our flight, and you know who graciously stepped up to the boarding agent and walked onto the plane. I looked back with a faint smile and said to myself, "I am glad I did what I did and fully cooperated. It seemed like an arduous process, but all things considered, it is better to be safe than sorry. They were just doing their jobs, and cooperation by all persons involved makes the transition so much easier." I followed Ginger on the plane and we headed home.

Reflective Thought

If we examine various scenarios in our lives that seem to be frustrating and bothersome, we would find one important factor. If we operate in the spirit of cooperation, we would avoid that added stress. There are times when we simply must cooperate in order to keep things moving along. For example, you arrive at a shopping center parking lot, and it is overflowing with other cars. You know, at some point, you will find a parking space and go on about your shopping. In order to get there, you need to cooperate with the other drivers in the lot. Everyone is looking for space, and you will simply have to cooperate with others until one becomes available. It would do you no good to start screaming and fussing with other people just because its crowded. It is one of those things in life you have to deal with. Your cooperation in the matter can make it that much easier or that much harder. I learned from my dog through patience and cooperation that the airport experience does not have to be a frustrating one. Abide in cooperation and goodwill, and you can make it through that situation and many others similar to it.

Ms. Ginger (my "ginger-snap")

References

(Scriptural references) The Holy Bible, KJV, Oral Roberts ed., Oral Roberts Evangelistic Association, Tulsa, OK, 1981

On Death and Dying, Elizabeth Kubler-Ross M.D., "What the Dying Have to Teach Doctors, Nurses, Clergy and Their Families," Scribner (a division of Simon & Schuster), New York, August 2014, retrieved March 2017 (chapter 7)

The Encyclopedia of Mammals, David McDonald (hardcover) Facts on File, November 1984 (Chapter 10)

Huffington Post, "30 Shocking Domestic Violence Statistics That Remind Us It's An Epidemic" by Alanna Vagianos, October 2014, retrieved December 2016, (chapter 11)

90395120R00085

Made in the USA
Columbia, SC
02 March 2018